# THE ADSENSE CODE

A STRATEGY

# JOEL COMM

## WHAT GOOGLE NEVER TOLD YOU ABOUT MAKING MONEY WITH ADSENSE

# THE ADSENSE CODE

ISBN: 1-933596-53-8 (Hardcover)

ISBN: 1-933596-70-8 (Paperback)

ISBN: 1-933596-71-6 (eBook)

**Published by:**

MORGAN · JAMES
THE ENTREPRENEURIAL PUBLISHER

Morgan James Publishing, LLC
1225 Franklin Ave Ste 325
Garden City, NY 11530-1693
Toll Free 800-485-4943
www.MorganJamesPublishing.com

**Habitat
for Humanity®**
Peninsula
Building Partner

**Interior Design by:**
Heather Kirk
www.GraphicsByHeather.com
Heather@GraphicsByHeather.com

*This book is dedicated to my wonderful family —
My beautiful wife, Mary, whom I have the privilege
of sharing my life with, Zach, my creative and
brilliant son, Jenna, who brightens any room she
walks into, and our dog, Socrates, whose furry
face and playful spirit bring joy to our home.*

# RAVE REVIEWS

"Joel, *The AdSense Code* is exactly what every AdSense publisher should have in the library. Most people only cover page creation and such, but you cover all of the things that actually make the difference between real profits and no profits.

One of the BEST info resources I've read so far and helped to open my eyes and pave my path way to bigger AdSense checks every month! Thanks for spilling the beans and keep the info coming."

~Raymond McNally, www.RaymondMcNally.com

"Joel's tips would have made me thousands of dollars and saved me dozens of hours if I had purchased *The AdSense Code* earlier. Even after spending two years learning things the hard way, I still found useful tips inside the book. If you want to become a successful AdSense publisher, buy this book."

~Will Spencer, www.Internet-Search-Engines-FAQ.com

"Joel's insights from over a decade of personal experience and rigorous testing of his ideas make *The AdSense Code* a bargain at twice the price. Joel is my income optimizing guru!"

~Greg Bulmash

"Joel's tips for increasing Google Adsense revenue are extraordinary! Being the lazy affiliate marketer that I am, I implemented only one of your tips and immediately DOUBLED my Adsense income. Then I didn't feel so lazy anymore, so I implemented another tip and TRIPLED the original sum. Two tips, triple the income... scary to think what might happen if I actually TRIED to make money with Adsense."

~Rosalind Gardner, www.NetProfitsToday.com

"Joel saved my business with a fraction of the insight found in *The AdSense Code*. Like many site operators, I had AdSense running on my site. It was doing 'okay.' Joel kicked it into high gear, and I will forever be in his debt."

~Chris Pirillo, www.LockerGnome.com

"This is the best book I've ever bought — my CTR was up 700% within a month. I'm now getting a new website up and running every three to four days! Earnings per day up from $3 to 5 to $30+. Making $900 per month extra for NO work seems like a good deal to me. I can't thank you enough!"

~Richard Allen

"I'd like to publicly thank Joel for helping to increase my adsense revenues from $1,000 a month to over $10,000 in less than 3 months (same traffic and everything). He answered all of my emails and gave me great suggestions after I purchased his course. I'm now living a semi-retired lifestyle at the ripe old age of 29. Thanks for changing my life!"

~Gary Fields

"Joel, I must confess that I was more than a bit skeptical before purchasing *The AdSense Code*. Boy, did you deliver the goods my friend! I had AdSense set up and running within 30 minutes of reading it, and the results are in — my revenue in the first 30 days was $1,800.83, which was more than enough to cover my mortgage payment! The next 30 days brought in over $2,200 in adsense income, so now my car payment is covered as well! Thanks Joel!"

~Michael Quick


"I purchased *The AdSense Code* a couple of days ago and have seen my AdSense revenue triple. It's amazing! Thank you."

~Gregg W.


"Before buying *The AdSense Code*, I was making about $50 a month. After reading your book and implementing several of the tips and strategies, however, my average has gone up to $800+ every month! Consider me a VERY satisfied customer."

~Gordy Seeley


"I've only just started using the techniques you describe and already I've seen a 600% increase in my CTR. You've definitely shown me what I need to do to start turning my virtual real-estate into a solid monthly revenue generator! THANK YOU!"

~Val from Canada

# ≡ INDEX ≡

RAVE REVIEWS . . . . . . . . . . . . . . . . . . . . . . . . . . . . . . . . . .v

LETTER FROM THE AUTHOR . . . . . . . . . . . . . . . . . . . . . .xvii

INTRODUCTION . . . . . . . . . . . . . . . . . . . . . . . . . . . . . . .xxi

1   GETTING STARTED WITH GOOGLE ADSENSE . . . . . . . . .1

    *1.1   THE BASICS: BUILDING YOUR SITE . . . . . . . . . . . . .3*

    *1.2   NAMING YOUR SITE . . . . . . . . . . . . . . . . . . . . . .3*

    *1.3   CHOOSING A HOSTING SERVICE . . . . . . . . . . . . . . .4*

    *1.4   DESIGNING THE SITE . . . . . . . . . . . . . . . . . . . . . .5*

    *1.5   CREATING CONTENT . . . . . . . . . . . . . . . . . . . . . .5*

    *1.6   SEARCH ENGINE OPTIMIZATION . . . . . . . . . . . . . . .6*

    *1.7   LINKS . . . . . . . . . . . . . . . . . . . . . . . . . . . . . . .6*

    *1.8   ADSENSE — MAKING THE MONEY! . . . . . . . . . . . . .7*

    *1.9   GOOGLE POLICIES . . . . . . . . . . . . . . . . . . . . . . .7*

    *1.10  AS EASY AS 1-2-3! . . . . . . . . . . . . . . . . . . . . . . .8*

2   HOW TO "TWEAK" YOUR ADS TO MAKE THEM "CLICK"! . . .11

    *2.1   AD FORMATS: "DRESS" YOUR ADS FOR SUCCESS! . . .13*

    *2.2   DON'T "LOOK" LIKE AN AD . . . . . . . . . . . . . . . . .13*

    *2.3   MEET THE ADSENSE FAMILY . . . . . . . . . . . . . . . .14*

    *2.4   TEXT ADS — GOOGLE'S FINEST . . . . . . . . . . . . . .15*

    *2.5   IMAGE ADS — BUILT TO BE IGNORED . . . . . . . . . .22*

    *2.6   LINK UNITS — GREAT LITTLE STOCKING FILLERS . . .23*

    *2.7   EXPANDED TEXT ADS — SHRINKING CONTROL*
          *OR EXPANDED INCOME? . . . . . . . . . . . . . . . . . . .29*

3   USING COLORS TO INCREASE YOUR CLICKS .......33

   *3.1   DESIGN YOUR WEBSITE TO HIGHLIGHT ADSENSE ...35*

   *3.2   MAKE THE BORDER GO! .......................36*

   *3.3   TEXT IS DESIGN TOO! ........................39*

   *3.4   BLUE IS BEST .............................40*

   *3.5   WHERE DID MY URL GO? ....................41*

   *3.6   DELIBERATE MISMATCHING .................41*

4   HOW TO MAXIMIZE VISIBILITY AND RESPONSE .....43

   *4.1   AD PLACEMENT: WHERE TO PUT YOUR ADS? .....45*

   *4.2   GO WITH THE 'FLOW' .......................45*

   *4.3   ABOVE THE FOLD .........................47*

   *4.4   USING TABLES ............................48*

   *4.5   COMPLEMENTING YOUR ADS ..................50*

5   CONTROLLING YOUR ADS .......................53

   *5.1   ATTRACTING RELEVANT ADS ..................55*

   *5.2   KEEP THE TITLE, DIRECTORY AND HEADLINES RELEVANT ...............................55*

   *5.3   FINDING KEYWORDS ........................56*

   *5.4   KEYWORD DENSITY .........................57*

   *5.5   KEYWORD PLACEMENT ......................57*

   *5.6   KEYWORD FRAMES .........................58*

   *5.7   SECTION TARGETING .......................59*

   *5.8   NO 'BAITING'! ...........................60*

   *5.9   CHANGING METATAGS .......................61*

   *5.10   INVITING THE ROBOT ......................61*

   *5.11   PUBLIC SERVICE ADS ......................61*

   *5.12   BLOCKING ADS ...........................63*

5.13   *"ADVERTISE ON THIS SITE"* .................... *63*

5.14   *DOES LOCATION MATTER FOR CPM ADS?* ....... *69*

6   CATCH FICKLE VISITORS WITH THE GOOGLE
SEARCH BOX ..................................... 71

6.1   *FINDING MONEY WITH SEARCH* ................ *73*

6.2   *LEARN HOW TO ADD GOOGLE SEARCH TO
YOUR WEB PAGE* ............................ *74*

6.3   *TO SEARCH OR NOT TO SEARCH* ............... *75*

6.4   *HOME PAGE SEARCHING* ...................... *76*

6.5   *CUSTOMIZING YOUR SEARCH* .................. *76*

7   ADSENSE AND FIREFOX REFERRAL PROGRAMS ...... 79

7.1   *REFERRING FOR ADSENSE* .................... *81*

7.2   *FIRING UP FIREFOX* .......................... *83*

8   USING MULTIPLE AD BLOCKS ....................... 85

8.1   *HOW MANY ADS IS TOO MANY?* ................ *87*

8.2   *WHAT TO DO WITH THREE AD UNITS* ........... *88*

8.3   *WHERE TO PUT THE SEARCH BOXES* ........... *89*

8.4   *GOOGLE IS MEAN WITH THE LINK UNITS* ....... *89*

8.5   *PUT REFERRAL BUTTONS NEAR AD UNITS* ....... *89*

8.6   *PUTTING IT ALL TOGETHER* ................... *90*

8.7   *PUTTING MULTIPLE ADS IN ARTICLES* .......... *90*

8.8   *PUTTING MULTIPLE ADS IN BLOGS* ............. *91*

8.9   *PUTTING MULTIPLE ADS IN MERCHANT SITES* ....*92*

9   BUILDING CONTENT ................................ 95

9.1   *WRITING CONTENT* .......................... *97*

9.2   *MAKING BUCKS WITH BLOGS* ................. *98*

9.3     ADDING ADSENSE TO YOUR BLOG . . . . . . . . . . . . . .99

9.4     OLD CONTENT . . . . . . . . . . . . . . . . . . . . . . . . . . . .101

9.5     VOLUNTEER WRITERS . . . . . . . . . . . . . . . . . . . . . . .104

9.6     BUILD THOUSANDS OF PAGES WITH OTHER
        PEOPLE'S CONTENT . . . . . . . . . . . . . . . . . . . . . . . . .105

9.7     ADD PUBLIC DOMAIN WORKS TO YOUR SITE . . . .108

9.8     ADSENSE IN RSS FEEDS . . . . . . . . . . . . . . . . . . . . . .110

9.9     USE YOUR NEWSLETTER TO DRIVE TRAFFIC! . . . .111

9.10    BUYING CONTENT/ HIRING WRITERS . . . . . . . . . . .112

9.11    AUTOMATED CONTENT . . . . . . . . . . . . . . . . . . . . . .112

10   RESPONSE TRACKING: YOUR HIDDEN POT OF
      ADSENSE GOLD! . . . . . . . . . . . . . . . . . . . . . . . . . . . .115

10.1    HOW TO TRACK WITH CHANNELS . . . . . . . . . . . . .119

10.2    HOW TO CREATE A CHANNEL . . . . . . . . . . . . . . . .120

10.3    HOW TO READ YOUR SERVER LOGS . . . . . . . . . . .123

10.4    TRACKING TOOLS . . . . . . . . . . . . . . . . . . . . . . . . . .128

11   SMART PRICING... AND WHAT IT MEANS FOR
      YOUR INCOME . . . . . . . . . . . . . . . . . . . . . . . . . . . . .133

11.1    WHAT GOOGLE HAS SAID ABOUT SMART
        PRICING . . . . . . . . . . . . . . . . . . . . . . . . . . . . . . . . . .136

11.2    WHAT ELSE DO WE KNOW ABOUT SMART
        PRICING? . . . . . . . . . . . . . . . . . . . . . . . . . . . . . . . . .137

11.3    STRATEGIES TO BENEFIT FROM SMART PRICING . . .138

12   HOW TO MAKE ADSENSE WORK WITH INTERNET
      COMMUNITIES . . . . . . . . . . . . . . . . . . . . . . . . . . . . .141

12.1    GOOGLE'S FORUM HEAT MAP . . . . . . . . . . . . . . . .144

13  HOW TO READ YOUR VISITORS LIKE A BOOK . . . . . . .149

    *13.1  MAKING SENSE OF STATS, LOGS AND REPORTS . . . . .151*

    *13.2  THE MOST IMPORTANT STAT OF ALL . . . . . . . . . . .151*

    *13.3  OPTIMUM CTR . . . . . . . . . . . . . . . . . . . . . . . .152*

    *13.4  ADSENSE ARBITRAGE . . . . . . . . . . . . . . . . . . . .152*

    *13.5  WORDTRACKER . . . . . . . . . . . . . . . . . . . . . . . .154*

14  WHAT TO DO BEFORE YOU APPLY TO
GOOGLE ADSENSE  . . . . . . . . . . . . . . . . . . . . . . . . . . . .157

    *14.1  DON'T BUILD A WEBSITE THAT SPECIFICALLY
    TARGETS SEARCH SPIDERS, WITH NOTHING UNIQUE
    TO OFFER HUMAN VISITORS. . . . . . . . . . . . . . . . . .160*

    *14.2  DON'T BUILD A WEBSITE JUST TO MAKE
    MONEY FROM ADSENSE . . . . . . . . . . . . . . . . . . . .160*

    *14.3  PROVIDE TARGETED CONTENT THAT WILL
    HELP GOOGLE ADVERTISERS TO CAPITALIZE
    YOUR TRAFFIC . . . . . . . . . . . . . . . . . . . . . . . . .160*

    *14.4  DON'T BUILD A WEBSITE SPECIFICALLY TO
    TARGET HIGH-VALUE KEYWORDS UNLESS YOU
    PLAN ON DEVELOPING QUALITY CONTENT! . . . . .161*

    *14.5  WEBSITES THAT RANK HIGHER IN A GOOGLE
    SEARCH (SERPS) WILL GET A BETTER PER-CLICK
    PAYOUT THAN WEBSITES WHICH RANK LOWER FOR
    THE SAME SEARCH TERM  . . . . . . . . . . . . . . . . . .162*

    *14.6  INCREASE 'READINESS TO BUY' . . . . . . . . . . . . . . .162*

    *14.7  DON'T CUT CORNERS! . . . . . . . . . . . . . . . . . . . .164*

15  RECOMMENDED RESOURCES: TRY THESE TOOLS
AND ADSENSE UTILITIES (SOME ARE FREE!)  . . . . . . . .165

    *15.1  TEST YOUR METTLE WITH THE ADSENSE
    SANDBOX! . . . . . . . . . . . . . . . . . . . . . . . . . . . . . .167*

**INDEX**    **xiii**

15.2    GOOGLE ADSENSE PREVIEW TOOL ............168

15.3    OVERTURE BIDTOOL .........................168

15.4    OVERTURE KEYWORD SUGGESTION TOOL .....169

15.5    ULTIMATE SEO TOOL ........................169

15.6    GOOGLE ADWORDS TRAFFIC ESTIMATOR
       AND BID TOOL ..............................169

15.7    KEYWORD RANKINGS TOOL ...................169

15.8    MASS KEYWORDS SEARCH ....................170

15.9    GUIDE TO GOOGLE-FRIENDLY DESIGN ........170

16   KEEPING TRACK OF WHAT WORKS — AND WHAT
DOESN'T WORK — FOR YOU! ......................171

    16.1    A SAMPLE ADSENSE JOURNAL .................175

17   OTHER CONTEXTUAL ADVERTISING PROGRAMS ....179

    17.1    KONTERA — MAKING YOUR WORDS PAY .......181

    17.2    CHITIKA — ALL MALLS, MORE MONEY .........182

    17.3    CONTEXTCASH — AFFILIATE REVENUE
           THE EASY WAY .............................183

    17.4    YAHOO! PUBLISHER NETWORK ................184

    17.5    ADBRITE .................................185

    17.6    KANOODLE — BRIGHT ADS ...................186

    17.7    SEARCHFEED ..............................186

18   GETTING TRAFFIC TO YOUR WEB SITE .............189

    18.1    ADVERTISING .............................191

    18.2    RECIPROCAL LINKING ......................192

    18.3    SEND A FRIEND ...........................193

    18.4    OFFLINE MARKETING .......................193

    18.5    PROMOTING YOUR BLOG ....................193

18.6    PUBLIC RELATIONS AND PUBLICITY . . . . . . . . . . .*194*

18.7    LEARN FROM A PRO . . . . . . . . . . . . . . . . . . . . . . . . .*196*

19   SEARCH ENGINE OPTIMIZATION . . . . . . . . . . . . . . . . . . . .197

19.1    ROBOT.TXT . . . . . . . . . . . . . . . . . . . . . . . . . . .*199*

19.2    TITLES AND URLS . . . . . . . . . . . . . . . . . . . . . . . .*200*

19.3    LINKS . . . . . . . . . . . . . . . . . . . . . . . . . . . . . . . .*200*

19.4    CREATE GATEWAYS . . . . . . . . . . . . . . . . . . . . . .*202*

19.5    AUTOMATIC SUBMISSIONS . . . . . . . . . . . . . . . . .*202*

19.6    SEO TOOLS . . . . . . . . . . . . . . . . . . . . . . . . . . . .*203*

19.7    A WORD ABOUT CLOAKING . . . . . . . . . . . . . . . . .*205*

20   ADSENSE NO-NOS . . . . . . . . . . . . . . . . . . . . . . . . . . . . . .207

20.1    WHAT TO DO IF YOUR ADSENSE ACCOUNT
          GETS CLOSED . . . . . . . . . . . . . . . . . . . . . . . . . . . .*212*

21   STAYING UP TO DATE AND LEARNING THE
     LATEST ADSENSE TIPS . . . . . . . . . . . . . . . . . . . . . . . . . . .213

22   CASE STUDIES . . . . . . . . . . . . . . . . . . . . . . . . . . . . . . . .217

22.1    FREEAFTERREBATE.INFO — UNMISSABLE ADS . . . . .*219*

22.2    GREAT IDEAS FOR INTEGRATION FROM
          THE IDEA BOX . . . . . . . . . . . . . . . . . . . . . . . . . . .*220*

22.3    GIFTS-911.COM GETS EMERGENCY TREATMENT
          WITH MULTIPLE AD UNITS . . . . . . . . . . . . . . . . . .*221*

22.4    STELLAAWARDS — A PRIZE WINNING DESIGN . . . . . .*223*

CONCLUSION . . . . . . . . . . . . . . . . . . . . . . . . . . . . . . . . . . . . .225

FOR OUR READERS . . . . . . . . . . . . . . . . . . . . . . . . . . . . . . . .229

LEGALESE . . . . . . . . . . . . . . . . . . . . . . . . . . . . . . . . . . . . . .231

# LETTER FROM THE AUTHOR

Dear Reader...

**Hidden on the Internet, scattered among billions of Web pages, are the clues to an incredible secret.**

For those who know the secret, the result is untold wealth. Each month, a small group of people — an elite club who have uncovered the mysteries of the AdSense Code and installed it on their websites — put their knowledge to use... and receive checks for tens of thousands of dollars from the people at Google.

Browse the Internet, find the right websites, analyze the ads and you can discover how members of that select group use their knowledge of the AdSense Code to generate huge wealth. You can find their secrets buried in the composition of their ads, hidden in their choice of colors and transformed by their choice of subject matter.

*This is an advanced book about Google AdSense that reveals the secrets of the AdSense Code.*

In writing this book I have assumed that you, the reader, have a basic knowledge of AdSense.

Don't let that scare you, because this book is simple to understand. If you are new to AdSense though, you might want to check out Google's AdSense Support Pages or occasionally refer to their online Glossary.

I have tried to keep this book concise and very focused on the objective of revealing the secrets of the AdSense Code and increasing your AdSense income. In this book you will find hands-on solutions to many of the concerns and challenges faced by content publishers in their quest to **attract targeted traffic, improve content relevance** and

**increase responsiveness to AdSense ads** — using easy and legitimate techniques that have worked for me and many others.

No matter what type of website you have or the nature of your content, you will find hands-on ways to increase your AdSense income.

Through the pages of this book, I will teach you the exact-same techniques that I used to create a TEN-FOLD increase in my AdSense earnings — almost overnight! Techniques that you can apply yourself and see real results.

To those of you expecting a fat Dummies-style book with entire chapters devoted to "What the heck is AdSense?" or "A brief history of contextual advertising" this slim manual might come as a bit of a surprise. But there's a reason for that. And the reason is that I don't want to lose you before you get to the real meaty parts. I will disclose, for the first time, my proven step-by-step techniques to increase your AdSense click-throughs.

Isn't that the real reason you bought this book?

If so, you won't be disappointed.

I don't want to hide these golden nuggets of wisdom under piles of fluff that you can read for free on the Internet. In fact, if you want to brush up on the basics, there's nothing like Google's own quick guide to AdSense, available at *www.Google.com/services/adsense_tour/*.

You might want to print it out into and have it handy. Refer to it often, or whenever in doubt. Why pay for free content! Get the basics direct from Google!

That doesn't mean that there's nothing in this book to help beginners though. In this revised edition, I have added a short section at the beginning for people who are just getting started. If you don't have a website, I'll tell you how to build one, get it online and start earning with AdSense fast. If you're already online and using AdSense — but want to know how to use it to earn much, much more — you can just skip straight past those pages and dive right into the gold! That's because getting set up with Google AdSense is the easy part. The harder part is making real money with it. And that's where this book comes in!

You'll also find some chapters on search engine optimization, traffic acquisition, content writing, ad formats and a whole host of other useful techniques that you can implement and feel the results in your pocket right away. I guarantee you will find insights here that you wouldn't find anywhere else.

My AdSense story — right from the sluggish $3/day times to the explosive $600/day — when AdSense pays off my mortgage, car payment, cable (and a whole lot more actually)… has taught me a great deal about how to make my web pages more profitable.

Every page is bursting with hard to-find AdSense tips, tricks and proven strategies — gleaned from successful publishers who have very generously shared their money-making ideas with me.

Put it all together and you too will know all the secrets of the AdSense Code.

**Read. Apply. And don't forget to report your results!**

Drop me an email anytime at *Joel.Comm@Adsense-Secrets.com.* I like to see these ideas 'at work'!

In the rapidly evolving world of contextual advertising, your unique problems and real-life results will help subsequent editions stay current and useful. I appreciate your inputs!

Yours for more AdSense Profits,

Joel Comm

# ⸬ INTRODUCTION ⸬

## *How To Make More Money With Google AdSense*

Google wants a slice of your traffic. And they're willing to pay big bucks!

For those who have been complaining of high traffic and low sales, there's simply no better way to cash in on those hard-earned visitors to your web pages.

## *AdSense Makes It So Easy!*

There's no complicated software to install, no need to scout for affiliates, nothing to buy and no need to even have a merchant account. So...

Why isn't everybody doing this? More importantly, why isn't everybody making the most of it?

## *It's "Hidden Money"*

"Seeing is believing", they say. Most webmasters love to obsessively track their visitors, earnings and CTR's several times a day. They love to see what's there, but they often miss what can be.

AdSense doesn't give you ultimate control over which ads are served, how the ads are rotated or what each click is worth. That's a good thing, because it's hands-free income. (It does give you some control though, and I'll tell you how to use those controls in this book.)

But many webmasters still think that once you've stuck the AdSense code on your page, there's little you can do except wait and watch.

**Nothing could be further from the truth!** Google gives you a great deal of control over your ads, and especially their visual or graphic elements. By tweaking these elements to your advantage, you could easily — in as little as a few minutes — multiply your click-throughs many, many times over!

## My Experiments With AdSense

I signed up with AdSense in June 2003, starting small by serving AdSense off just a few of my pages.

By the end of the day, I'd delivered several thousand AdSense impressions — which netted me the princely sum of... $3.00. I didn't exactly burn down the house.

While I didn't see a great deal of potential based on this initial figure, I figured it couldn't hurt to place AdSense code on more pages.

Over the period of a couple months, I increased my impressions 25-fold, but the clicks just weren't happening. That was when I hit my lowest point as an Internet publisher. My click-through ratios were so bad, I needed thousands of visitors to net about $30 per day.

At that point, I knew something had to change — and I was going to change it!

It was as late as April 2004 — ten months after I signed up with AdSense — that I had my eyes opened to what I had been missing all along. It was one of the "Ah-Ha!" moments where I felt as though I was being hit by the proverbial two-by-four. Immediately, I began experimenting with my Google ads, testing various placement and colors to see if my assumptions would hold water.

### The results were fast — and fantastic!

By applying the same easy tweaks discussed in this book, I nearly tripled my click-through rate, and my income shot up to $600 PER DAY! I still remember that golden day in April 2004 — and for me there's been no looking back.

From my early days of being an "AdSense nobody" to becoming a leading AdSense guru, when a five-figure monthly income no longer surprises me... it's been an eventful journey full of learning experiences.

## Little cogs run the AdSense machinery!

It's easy to get carried away when you're making so much money. But I never lose sight of the little things that make me big money with AdSense.

Every AdSense partner — however big or small — knows that at the end of the day, it all boils down to one thing: stats! Your AdSense stats might not be amazing to start with, but make it a habit to go through it with a fine-toothed comb. As you start making sense of those 'little numbers'... the big checks will follow!

| | |
|---|---|
| Monday, November 7, 2005 | $626.50 |
| Tuesday, November 8, 2005 | $672.00 |
| Wednesday, November 9, 2005 | $638.70 |
| Thursday, November 10, 2005 | $634.12 |
| Friday, November 11, 2005 | $590.31 |
| Saturday, November 12, 2005 | $608.31 |
| Sunday, November 13, 2005 | $667.64 |
| Monday, November 14, 2005 | $815.42 |
| Tuesday, November 15, 2005 | $789.00 |

Stats are the holy grail of Internet Marketing. This is a real, recent screenshot of my AdSense stats page. You can see what I'm making daily, but specific details such as CPM and CTR have been blacked out in keeping with Google's terms of service.

### Hitting the AdSense Jackpot!

As you can see, today AdSense takes care of my car payment, mortgage, cable bills and a whole lot more besides.

### Aren't you dying to know...

WHAT was it I did to AdSense — and my website — that turned it overnight into a cash-cow on steroids?!

More importantly, what can YOU do to shoot your AdSense income through the roof- right NOW!

## *My Advice To You Is Quite Simple...*

Don't be passive about your AdSense income; work hard to increase it. But before you try out that hot new idea you read about at an Internet Forum, be sure to check out Google's AdSense TOS at *Google.com/adsense/localized-terms.* Some web publishers have forever relinquished their fat AdSense paychecks, just because they were too busy to pay attention to something so fundamental to their AdSense survival.

I like to <u>play by the rules</u> and have taken adequate care to ensure that my AdSense tips and tweaks are legit. Making what I do from AdSense, I have little incentive to go on a rule-breaking spree and get my AdSense account suspended.

For many Internet site owners, AdSense is like the goose that lays the golden egg. Take good care of your goose — don't slaughter it in the mad rush to increase your AdSense income!

# *CHAPTER*

# *1*

# Getting Started With
# Google AdSense

# GETTING STARTED WITH GOOGLE ADSENSE

## 1.1 The Basics: Building Your Site

I regularly receive email from people asking how they can get started in making money with AdSense. I'm always happy to help people make the most of Google, but many of these people didn't even have a website!

Here's the bad news: to make money with AdSense, you've got to have a website. There's no getting around that. The good news though is that it's never been easier to create a website from scratch and use it to generate real revenue.

I'm going to give a brief introduction here to creating a website from the ground up. You can find plenty more information online and I'll tell you where to look. A good place to start is my own book How To Build Profitable Websites Fast, available at *www.BuildAWebsiteFast.com.*

If you already have a site up and running, you can just skip this bit, head down to 1.10 and begin reading about how to improve your AdSense revenues.

## 1.2 Naming Your Site

The first thing your site will need is a name. That's easier said than done these days. All the best words in the dictionary have either already been bought and built by developers or they've been bought and offered by speculators.

But that doesn't mean you can't create a good name and buy it for a song. Putting two words together with a hyphen can work (like *www.adsense-*

*tools.com*) and there are plenty of good names available if you're prepared to move outside the world of .coms into .net and .biz etc.

Your first stop should be *www.NetworkSolutions.com*. This is a nuts and bolts service that lets you hunt and buy names, order hosting plans and even submit your site to the search engines. When you're looking for a name, you can just toss in ten options and the site will tell you which (if any) are available. Find a good one, and you can either buy it there or pick it up at *www.godaddy.com* (they can be a bit cheaper). All in, buying a name from one of these services won't cost you more than about $5 a year.

If you can't find a name you like and that hasn't already been grabbed, you can take a look at sites like moderndomains.com and bestnames.net. These are companies that buy domain names and sell them for a profit. There's a good chance you'll find some good names here but they can cost you anywhere from $50 to $50,000. Before you part with a penny, think about the advantage that a good name can bring and ask yourself if you can't get the extra traffic a cheaper way. Often, you can.

## 1.3 Choosing A Hosting Service

Your site is going to be stored on a hosting company's server. (You didn't want thousands of people dialing into your computer every hour, did you?) Again, there are lots of different options available depending on how much you want to pay and what you need.

In general, you'll want to make sure that you have about 50 megabytes of space (that's enough for 100 pages!), full statistics reporting and most importantly, 24 hour service. If your site goes down, you'll be losing money every hour it's offline. If there's a problem with the server, you want to make sure it's fixed right away.

You get what you pay for with Web hosting from "free" services that will cost you more than you save to $200 a month for dedicated servers. Twenty bucks a month is a reasonable price to pay and GoDaddy.com and NetworkSolutions.com both offer good programs.

## 1.4 Designing The Site

It used to be said that absolutely anyone could create a website. That was true: absolutely anyone who knew HTML. Today, you don't even need to know that. Programs like Microsoft's FrontPage or NVU (which is free; you can download it at *www.nvu.com*) let you create sites without needing to know your tags from your tables. If you can use Word, you can create a website.

You can either have fun playing with the programs and designing the site yourself or you can hire a professional designer to do it for you.

Freelance sites like *www.elance.com* and *www.guru.com* are good places to advertise. You can invite designers to give you quotes and pick the best based on price and talent. Be sure to check feedback and portfolios though; a low bid is often low for a good reason.

## 1.5 Creating Content

In Chapter 9, I talk in detail about building content and optimizing what you write to attract traffic and maximize your AdSense revenues. There are all sorts of ways to do that but for the moment just bear in mind that the ads that appear on your site will depend on the content on your pages. That's how AdSense works: users click on the ads because they're relevant.

And that's why it's not worth putting up a site just to cash in on particular keywords. Google doesn't like it and neither do users. If your site doesn't genuinely interest your visitors, you'll find it hard to get traffic, links and clicks on your ads.

But there are still a lot of different ways to create content very easily that improves your income. I'll tell you all about them in Chapter 9.

It's also worth remembering that Google doesn't place ads on particular types of sites, so if you're thinking of building a casino site stuffed with AdSense ads, you can forget about it; it's not going to happen.

Before you build a site that contains any content that's remotely controversial, check out the Terms of Service (TOS) to make sure that it's allowed. It will tell everything you need to know.

## 1.6 Search Engine Optimization

Of course, once you're up, people have to know you're there. One of the most important ways to do that is get yourself a high-ranking in a search engine.

There are lots of different search engines, but only three are really important: Google, Yahoo! and MSN. In **chapter 17**, I'll talk in more detail about improving your search engine rankings.

If you want to take a shortcut, there are plenty of companies which will make the submissions for you and they'll even optimize your site to get you as high on the rankings as possible.

## 1.7 Links

Your search engine ranking will depend on a number of factors. One of those factors is the number of sites that link to yours. As far as Google is concerned if lots of sites about model railways link to your model railway site that must be a pretty good sign that people who like model railways think your site is good. So they'll want to offer it to people who search for model railways, bringing you lots of free traffic.

Once you've got your site up and running you'll want to persuade other sites to give you links. You could offer to exchange links and you can even set up a page that contains recommended links so that you'll have somewhere to put them.

There's a range of other strategies and services that you can use. You can find out about those in chapter 19 too.

## 1.8  AdSense — Making The Money!

Once you've done all this, you'll be ready to start using — and prof-iting from — AdSense. The application process is very simple and straightforward.

First, you'll have to tell Google whether you're a company or a one-man show. That's important because it tells them where to send the money. (In general, it's better to get your money by direct deposit; Google charges for express mail checks.) You'll also have to choose whether you want content-based ads, search ads or both. (Content-based ads are better but I'll tell you how to benefit from each.)

Once you're approved, you'll just have to copy and paste a small piece of code into your website and you're done!

## 1.9  Google Policies

AdSense works. I know it works because I've got the stats, the checks and the bank balance to prove it. And all of the methods that I used to increase my AdSense revenues were completely legitimate and in line with Google's policies.

That's important. It is possible to cheat AdSense. But you'd have to be crazy to do it. You can make so much money working within Google's rules that to risk getting thrown out by putting ads on pages without content or by persuading users to click on the ads is just plain crazy.

You can find an excellent run-down of Google's do's and don'ts (mostly don'ts) at *Google.com/adsense/policies* and I've put a more detailed list at the back of this book. The things to look out for in particular are:

### Code Modification

You have to paste the AdSense code onto your site as is. And you don't need to do anything else! Your AdSense account will let you play with colors and placements (and getting that right is what will really rocket your income) so why bother playing with Google's HTML? It's not necessary and it could get you a lifetime ban.

### Incentives

When the ads appear on your page, you have to leave them completely alone. You might be tempted to tell your users to "click here" or support your sponsors but if Google catches you, they could well cut you off. They want people to click because they're genuinely interested in the ad. Get your strategy right and they'll do just that.

### Content

Google is pretty picky about where the ads are displayed. They don't want advertisers complaining to them that their services were being promoted on a site that supports gambling or is filled with profanity or contains more ads than content. If your content doesn't come up to scratch, you'll need a site that does.

### Prohibited Clicks

And nastiest of all are the people who either click on their own ads or create programs to do it for them.

The bottom line is that you don't need any of this stuff. Maximizing your revenue *within the rules* is easy!

## 1.10  As Easy as 1-2-3!

The bottom line is that there are three ways to increase your AdSense revenue.

1.  **By Tweaking the Ads** to make them more appealing to your visitors;

2.  **By Optimizing your Website** for better AdSense targeting (or what the Google folks call 'content relevance');

And the only sure-fire way to get 1 and 2 right is by...

### 3. Tracking Visitor Response.

If you don't know what works (and what doesn't work) in trying to increase your AdSense revenue... you're shooting arrows in the dark!

The right tracking tools can reveal a great deal about your visitors and answer fundamental questions such as **what they're looking for** and **what makes them 'click'**. Once you've figured that out, bingo! You're on your way to big AdSense bucks!

But it isn't as straight-forward as it seems. If it were, there wouldn't be so many grumpy people on AdSense forums, complaining about their low AdSense earnings.

It's not that they aren't doing anything about it. They simply aren't doing the right things.

Let me assure you that in the time that I have been using AdSense, my earnings have only gone up — and so will yours, if you apply all my techniques seriously.

# *CHAPTER*
# 2

# How To "Tweak"
# Your Ads To Make
# Them "Click"!

# HOW TO "TWEAK" YOUR ADS TO MAKE THEM "CLICK"!

## 2.1 Ad Formats: "Dress" your ads for success!

How would you like your ads served? Banners? Skyscrapers? Rectangles? Squares? What about borders and background colors?

The choices can be overwhelming. Many people let Google decide for them- preferring to stick with the default settings. Big mistake! From my own experience I can tell you that it's like swapping a hundred-dollar bill for a ten-dollar one.

For almost one year I settled for just a tenth of what I could have been making — just because I didn't bother to control the looks and place-ment of my AdSense ads.

The various ad formats, colors and their placement on the web page can be done in thousands of combinations. You can literally spend hours every day experimenting with every possible combination. But you don't want to, do you?

Let me give you a few 'ground rules' that have sky-rocketed the CTR's on my top-grossing pages:

## 2.2 Don't "Look" Like An Ad

People don't visit your website for ads. They want good content.

If you make the ads stick out with eye-popping colors, images or borders, that makes them easy to recognize as ads — and people work extra hard to avoid them. The same goes for ads that are tucked away in the top, bottom or some other far corner of the page. So easy to ignore!

If you want people to click, make the ads look like an integral part of your content.

> *Today's visitors are blind to banners, mad at pop-ups, weary of ads and skeptical of contests and giveaways. So how do you win their confidence? Simple. Don't make your ads look like ads!*

Let's begin by reviewing each of the different types of ad available from AdSense and explaining their uses... then I'll introduce you to a few simple choices that zoomed my CTRs to incredible heights.

## 2.3 Meet the AdSense Family

Google serves its ads in three flavors, with each of those flavors coming in a range of different shapes and sizes. It is very important to understand the differences between each of these ads. Some are ideal for particular locations. Some should never be used in certain locations. And some should never be used at all.

The sample page at *Google.com/adsense/adformats* lets you see all of the different kinds of ads at once. It even has links to sample placements that demonstrate how the ads can be used.

For the most part, I'd recommend that you ignore those sample placements.

I'll talk about location in more detail later in the book, but for now just bear in mind that many of the ads in the samples are just too out of the way to be noticed.

You can use them as a starting point if you want but you'll save yourself a lot of time — and money — by taking advantage of the experience of myself and others, and following the recommendations here.

## 2.4 Text Ads — Google's Finest

Text ads are probably the types of ad that you're most familiar with. You get a box containing one or a number of ads with a linked headline, a brief description and a URL. You also get the "Ads by Google" notice that appears on all AdSense ads.

There are eight different types of text ad. The most popular is probably the **leaderboard**. At 728 x 90, it stretches pretty much across the screen and while it can be placed anywhere, it's mostly used at the top of the page, above the main text.

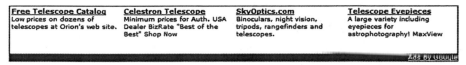

*Fig. 2.1 The leaderboard.*

That's a great location. It's the first thing the reader sees and it offers a good selection of ads to choose from. When you're just starting out and still experimenting with the types of ads that work best with your users, it's a pretty good default to begin with.

Of course, you can put it in other places too. Putting a leaderboard ad between forum entries for example can be a pretty good strategy sometimes and definitely worth trying. Though I think you'll probably find that one of the smaller ads, such as a banner or half-banner might blend in more there and bring better results.

And I think you can often forget about putting a leader board at the bottom of the page, despite what Google's samples show you. It would certainly fit there but you have to be certain that people are going to reach the bottom of the page, especially a long page. You might find that only a small minority of readers would get that far, so you're already reducing the percentage of readers who would click through.

Overall, I'd say that leaderboards are most effective blended into the top of the page beneath the navigation bar and sometimes placed between forum entries.

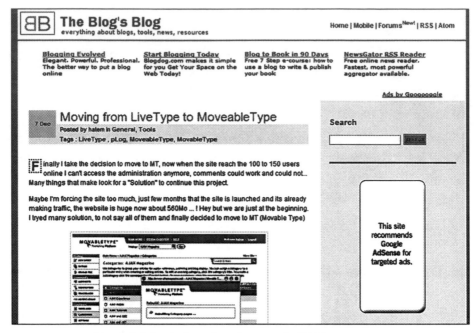

Fig. 2.2 A leaderboard at the top of PHPMagazine.net.

**Banners** (468 x 60) and **half-banners** (234 x 60) are much more flexible. Like leaderboards you can certainly put these sorts of ads at the top of the page, and lots of sites do it. Again, that's something worth trying. You can put up a leaderboard for a week or so, swap it for a banner for another week or so, and compare the results.

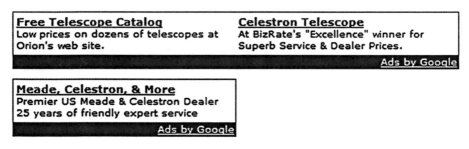

Fig. 2.3 A banner and a half-banner.

But at the top of the page, I'd expect the leaderboard to do better. A banner or a half-banner would leave too much space on one side and make the ad stand out. It would look like you've set aside an area of the page for advertising instead of for content. That would alert the reader that that section of the page is one that they can just ignore.

When you're looking for an ad to put in the middle of the page though, a half-banner can be just the ticket.

While a leaderboard will stretch over the sidebars of your site, just like the navigation bar, a 234 x 60 half-banner will fit neatly into the text space on most sites.

This sort of ad should be your default option for the end of articles and the bottom of blog entries.

*But for the most part, stay away from the 468 x 60 banner ad block!*

One of the first things people do when they sign up for AdSense is to grab a 468 x 60 ad block.

Big mistake.

I have a theory about why they do this. It's the same theory that explains why the 468 x 60 block does not entice clicks.

Most site owners have the mindset that when they put Google ads on their site, they must place the code that conforms most to traditional web advertising. And that would be...? Yup, the 468 x 60, the ubiquitous banner format that we have all come to know and love and... IGNORE.

Everyone is familiar with the 468 x 60. And that's exactly why the click-through rate on this size is very low, even among advertisers who use images on their banners.

The 468 x 60 blocks screams, "Hey! I am an advertisement! Whatever you do, DON'T click me. In fact, you should run from me as fast as you can!"

In all but a few special cases, I have found the 468 x 60 ad block to be completely ineffective, and recommend ignoring it the same way your visitors do.

Now, that doesn't mean you can never use it. You just have to know what you're doing and do it smartly. *You have to do everything you can to make sure that that ad block looks absolutely nothing like a traditional banner ad.*

At my site, WorldVillage.com, I've done that by surrounding the ad with text. Because there's no border around the unit, the ads blend into the text and look almost as they're a part of the article.

If I had left that unit in the middle of some empty space — at the top of the page for example — it would have looked exactly like the sort of banner that users have trained themselves to avoid. It wouldn't have picked up any clicks at all.

(Note, I could probably have used a half-banner here too but in general, I like to give my users as wide a choice of ads to click as possible.)

While this use of a 468 x 60 works for me — and it can work for you too if you blend it into the page properly — I'd stick to other formats, like the, half-banner if you're not 100 percent sure that you can pull it off.

When this ad unit fails, it can fail big.

**Diabetes, Recognizing the Signs, and Symptoms**
Posted in Health, Diabetes at 02:07 PM by Jay B Stockman

Discovering you have Diabetes is frightening, don't panic, people with Diabetes can live long, healthy, happy lives.

Continue reading "Diabetes, Recognizing the Signs, and Symptoms"

**Workplace Workouts**
Posted in Health, at 10:32 AM by Srinivas GS

Workplace, especially for computer professionals/operators, does bring in stress and fatigue. It is very important that we dont get tired and stressed during work hours. This is possible by following a few Healthy and easy methods to reduce tiredness while at work.

Continue reading "Workplace Workouts"

**Unique Christmas Gift Ideas For Teens**
Posted in Family, Teen Topics at 08:21 AM by Nathalie Lussier

Do you know someone who is picky and hard to shop for? Well if they think they're too cool for your gifts, why not find a better christmas gift for them this year? There are a lot of great christmas gifts out there just waiting to be picked up and sent off. So whether you're looking to buy your best friend, your boyfriend, your girlfriend or your brother and sister a nice christmas gift you're going to be able to find some unique gifts for them!

Continue reading "Unique Christmas Gift Ideas For Teens"

| **Christmas Gift Ideas** | **Unique Gifts under $30** |
| Directory of gift ideas. Find Christmas ideas quickly. | Free engraving and embroidery. Unique Gifts for family & friends. |
| Ads by Goooooogle | Advertise on this site |

*Fig. 2.4 Banner ads at WorldVillage.com. Note how the ad links come immediately after an article link so that the ads look like part of the site.*

Google also offers five different kinds of rectangular ads: **buttons** (125 x 125), **small rectangles** (180 x 150), **medium rectangles** (300 x 250), **large rectangles** (336 x 280), and **squares** (250 x 250).

In fact, all of the rectangles can be slotted into the same spots on the page... with the exception of the button.

Probably the most common use of rectangles is at the beginning of articles. You can wrap the text around the ad, forcing the reader to look at it if he wants to read the article. That's very effective.

But you can really put these sorts of ads anywhere on the page. On my site, DealOfDay.com, I've put two rectangular ads right at the top of the page so that they take up the bulk of the space the user sees before he starts to scroll. That's a very aggressive approach that might not work on every site. It's worth trying though because if it works for you, you can find that it brings in great revenues.

If you're wondering which size of ad would be best for the position you've got in mind, my advice is to start with the large rectangle, the 336 x 280.

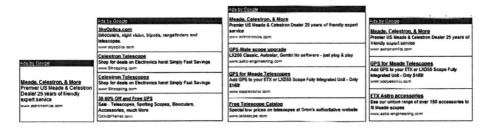

*Fig. 2.5 Small, medium and large rectangles... and the square.*

Why should you choose the 336 x 280 ad block? Simple. It gets the most clicks! My studies have shown that this format looks most like real content added to a page. I've dabbled with every size Google offers and this is the size that consistently has the best results. Other people have told me the exact same thing. That's all I need to know!

Second best is the 300 x 250 rectangle.

This ad block size is really useful when you went to have two sets of ads side by side. They fit on most web pages just perfectly.

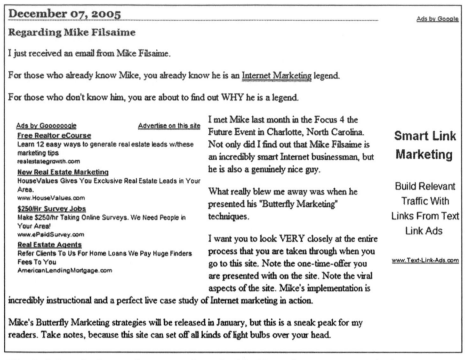

*Fig. 2.6 A typical use of a rectangle embedded into the text at www.joelcomm.com...*

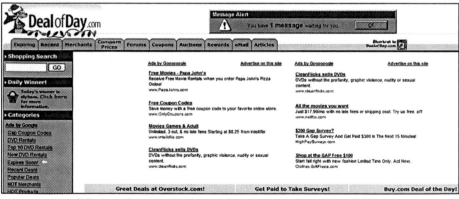

*Fig. 2.7 ... and an atypical use of two rectangles at Dealofday.com.*

**Buttons** should generally be used in a different way to other rectangles. Like the half-banners, they're distinctive for their small size.

While that means you could slot them in anywhere, I think they work best when slipped into the sidebars.

For example, you might have a list of links to frequently-read articles or other sites on one side of your page. Putting a button ad at the end of a list like that could help it to blend in well.

The final types of text ads are those that run vertically. These come in three sizes: **skyscraper** (120 x 600), **wide skyscraper** (160 x 600) and **vertical banner** (120 x 240).

Clearly, these are useful options for filling up the sides of the page.

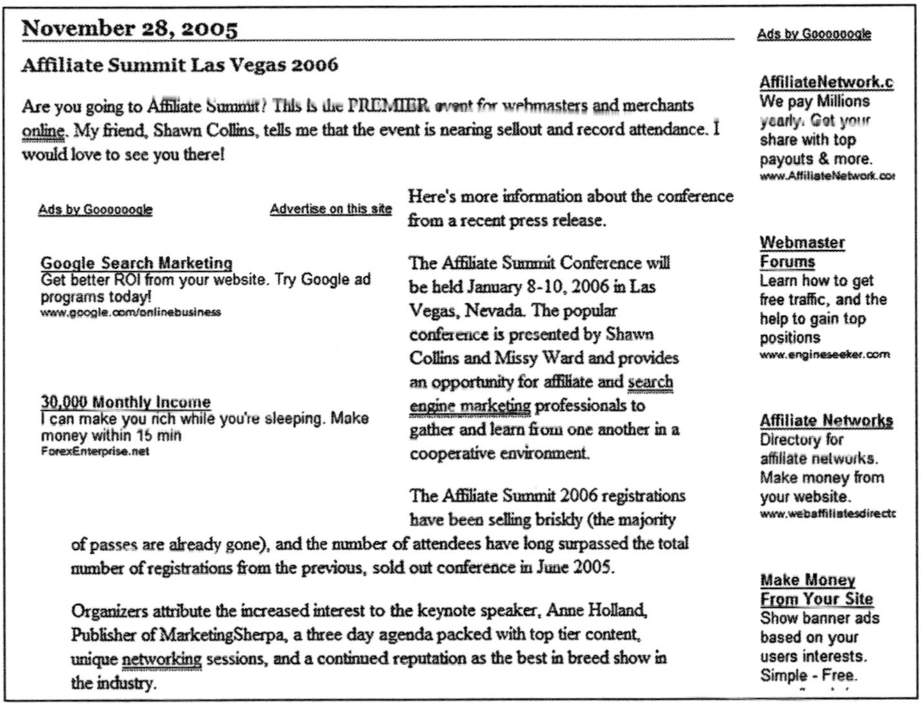

*Fig. 2.8 A skyscraper stretching down the right of the page at JoelComm.com.*

I would also recommend using the 'wide skyscraper', text-only ads on the right hand edge of the screen — in conjunction with the 3-way matching I talk about in chapter 3.

If you think about it, nearly all PC users are right handed (even left-handed people like me control their mouse with their right hand because it's how we were 'brought up' to use a mouse.) By placing the ads on the right hand edge it's psychologically 'less distance' between your right hand and the screen.

This 'closeness' in my opinion makes the user feel more comfortable and therefore more likely to click through to a link. They feel more in control of their visit experience.

Typically, you can often divide sites into those that have plenty of content at the sides (especially on some blogs), and those that have nothing on the sides (like at *JoelComm.com*).

I think putting vertical ads in space so that they form the border of the main text makes the page look a lot cleaner. But that doesn't necessarily mean that they're going to get more clicks. If you're putting a vertical banner in an area where you have other content then just make sure, as always, that you blend them in well so that they look like the rest of your content.

## 2.5 Image Ads — Built To Be Ignored

Text ads should always be your first pick when you start to load up your site. Image ads should always be your last choice.

A text ad offers many advantages over image ads:

A.  With the right formatting, a text ad 'blends in' with your site content. An image ad will not give you the same freedom with its appearance, as the only thing you can play with is the size and positioning.

B.  You can squeeze more text ads into the space that a conventional banner takes. People love to have more choices!

C.  Properly formatted text ads don't look like clutter. Banners do!

D.  People hate banners and avoid them at sight. Many tests confirm that people are much more receptive to text ads related with your content.

I just can't think of a reason why anyone would want to take an image ad from Google. Text ads perform so much better, in my opinion, you're better off sticking with those and ignoring image ads altogether.

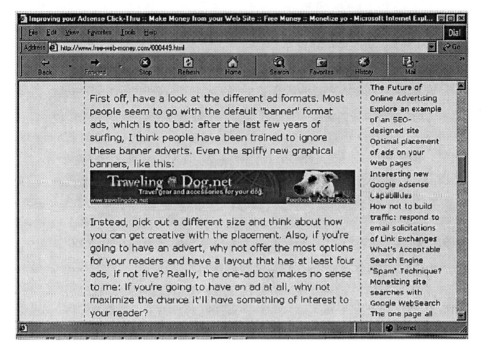

*Fig. 2.9 This banner ad stands out, but will it get clicked? Dave Taylor, best-selling technology writer and AdSense partner, stands up for text ads in this article at: www.Free-Web-Money.com/000449.html*

That doesn't mean you can't use images to subtly draw people click on ads. You can and I'll discuss how to do that later in this book. But images that are ads just scare people away.

## 2.6 Link Units — Great Little Stocking Fillers

If you've ever bought Christmas presents for children, you've probably bought stocking fillers. You dole out hundreds of bucks on some state-of-the-art electronic gizmo, toss in a couple of toy cars that cost a dollar each just to fill up space and give the kid more to unwrap... then watch him spend 90 percent of his time playing with the car that cost 10 percent of your total gift budget.

Ad Link units have the potential to be equally profitable.

They're very small, almost unnoticeable... but when used well, they can be extremely effective. Ad Link units let you place a box on your site that contains four or five links. They come in sizes ranging from 20 x 90 to 200 x 90, and are really meant to be placed on a sidebar.

Because you can place both Ad Link units as well as other ad units on the page, you might find that the choice helps: if a user doesn't spot something interesting in one type of ad block, he might spot it on another.

Where Ad Links differ from other types of ads is that they only display a list of topics that Google believes are relevant to the content of your pages. They don't display the ads themselves. When a visitor clicks on a topic, Google pops up a new window with targeted ads.

It can be argued that the Ad Links are ineffective because people have to go through two clicks in order for you to get paid. That's right, you only get paid for the second click (but that does mean you can check to see which ads your users are being served.)

But it can also be argued that if someone is taking the time to click on a topic, then they are probably very interested in the link, and are likely to click an actual advertisement on the resulting page. Some people have found that just about everyone who clicks on an Ad Link will click on the ads that appear on the next page.

I have tested Ad Links on multiple sites and have seen vast differences in results. That makes it more difficult to say whether or not they are for you. In the first case, I placed the Ad Links on an information-based site with a very general audience. The results were nothing to write home about. Let's just say that you could just about buy a large candy bar with the CPM I saw.

In the second case, I placed the Ad Links on a product specific site with a narrow audience. The results were fantastic! We're talking about a CPM that is greater than what someone might make flipping burgers in one day.

The conclusions should be obvious. If you're going to use Ad Links units campaign. You need to put them:

1. **On a site with a specific field of interest**. A general site will give you general ads — and few clicks.

2. **Above the fold with few other links**. For Ad Links, this is crucial: If your users are going to click a link, it should be a link that gives you money.

It's also a good idea to keep your Ad Link units for sites with high-paying keywords. If someone comes to your site seeking out information or a product on a top-notch keyword, they tend to be more likely to click as a result.

Let's take a look at an example:

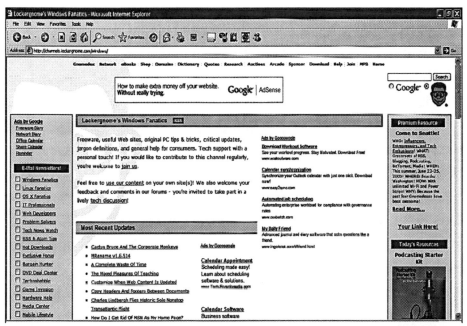

*Fig. 2.10 LockerGnome.com puts AdLinks above a list of links on the left so that they blend into the site.*

Chris Pirillo's site at Lockergnome.com is an excellent template for how to do AdSense properly. While I don't have access to his AdSense statistics, I have watched his sites long enough to speculate as to his success.

The center column of his page is classic AdSense placement. He is using a medium or large rectangle with blue links, black text and subtle URL. The ads are placed inline and right justified.

People start on the left and drift to the right. My testing has also shown that ads on the right perform best.

He is using a 120 x 600 skyscraper ad in sidebars, as many people do. Chris has also thought outside the box and used the white space next to his bullet points for this page. Right justifying the skyscraper block and placing it inline is a slick move.

But look where his Ad Links are: in the top left column of the page, above the fold. That means you can see Ads by Google as the first item. As long as those AdLinks are very targeted to the content on the page, they could generate 1 percent to 2 percent in clicks.

If you have the space and they fit in your sidebar, I would test them on your site as well.

There are two kinds of link units: **vertical units** and **horizontal units**. Chris Pirillo's site is a great example of the right way to use vertical link units.

But horizontal link units can be at least as effective. Since they were introduced, they really have become an extremely useful tool.

Some users have reported increases in CTR as high as 200 percent using these units!

Instead of piling the links one on top of the other-which is great for putting above lists of links but stand out too clearly when placed in text-the horizontal ads blend in perfectly when placed on pages with articles.

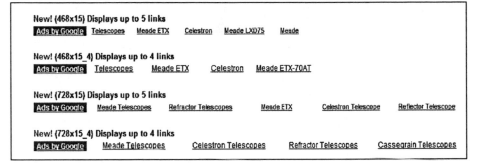

*Fig. 2.11 New horizontal Ad Link units are great for inserting into articles and show very clearly which keywords your site is generating.*

You can still only use one Ad Link unit per page and users still have to click twice before you get paid but they're definitely worth slipping into a long article.

You probably shouldn't put them at the bottom of a page where they'll be very easy to miss, but there are plenty of other places where these sorts of ads can work very, very well.

For example, a horizontal ad unit can be a great alternative to a leaderboard. It's much more subtle and takes up less space on the page — definitely something to experiment with to see which of the two brings you the highest revenues.

Or you could use them to separate forum or blog entries. As a horizontal unit, they can be very effective as frames that give people somewhere easy to go when they reach the end of a text unit.

One great use for horizontal link units though is on directory pages. If you have a Web page that contains tables of links, slipping a horizontal link unit above or below them — or both — can make the ads look like a part of the directory.

It almost makes you want to build a directory just to try it out!

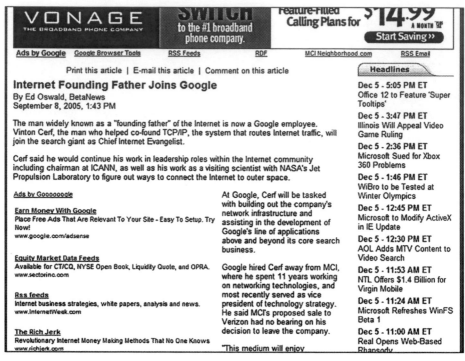

*Fig. 2.12 A horizontal link unit at the top of the page at BetaNews.com. Would a leaderboard have produced better revenues in that position? Again, something that can easily be tested.*

To sum up the different types of ad format then,

- **Leaderboards** are best at the top of the page
- **Squares and rectangles** can be embedded into text itself
- **Vertical ads and buttons** should slip down the side of the page
- **Vertical link units** should be placed next to link lists
- **Horizontal link units** can go at the top of the page between blog entries or above and below directories
- And **image ads** shouldn't be used at all

Those are the general rules governing ad formats. They're worth knowing because they're a good place to start.

They're also worth knowing because you can't break the rules until you know what they are... and that's when the fun really begins!

## 2.7 Expanded Text Ads — Shrinking Control Or Expanded Income?

Take a look at the ad format samples on the AdSense site and you'll see a bunch of squares and rectangles filled with ads. Most of those ad units will contain more than one ad. On those units that do contain just the one ad, like the button or the half-banner, the ad will fill the space neatly and look pretty subtle.

You might be surprised then to put a skyscraper or a leaderboard on your site and find just one giant ad, written in super-sized text.

All the effort you've put into picking the right ad for your site, testing to see which formats work best and calculating which will give you the most clicks will have gone right out of the window.

You've prepared your site to serve multiple ads that look like content, and instead you're handing out a single ad that just screams "Don't click me!"

This can happen sometimes, but it's not a reason to panic. It might even be a reason to celebrate.

There are two possible reasons that Google is sending you these expanded text ads.

The first possible reason is that you've been <u>keyword-targeted</u>. Google keeps track of your results (just like you should be doing) and tries to serve up the number of ads for your page that will bring in the highest amount of income. That might be four ads in a unit. Or just the one.

Frankly, I'm a touch skeptical that showing one ad is going to be bring me more revenues than showing several can do. But I'm prepared to give Google the benefit of the doubt.

If I see that Google is giving me one ad, I'll compare the results for that one ad to the previous results that I've had serving multiple ads in the same unit. If I find that my revenues have dropped I can either block that ad using my filters or just ask AdSense not to give me any more single ads.

But if I find that the expanded text ad is giving me more money, I might still be worried. I know that users are more likely to click ads that look like content. I also know that they prefer to have a choice of ads rather than just one option.

If I'm getting more clicks then with just one ad, it could well be that I'm doing something wrong with my ad unit. I would want to look at how well it's been optimized and whether it's in the right place to bring in the best income.

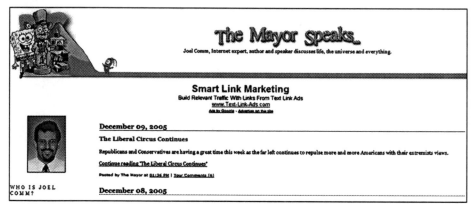

*Fig. 2.13 You can't miss that! An expanded text ad strikes JoelComm.com.*

It could well be that that one ad could be a high-payer and works better with little competition. But it could also be that getting one ad is a warning that something's wrong with the way you've laid out that ad unit on your site.

You might want to try some different strategies to see if they'll increase your revenues when the multiple ads come back.

There is another possibility though. You might have been site-targeted.

This is a whole different ball game. It means that an advertiser has spotted your site and asked Google to run their ads on it on a **pay-per-impression** basis.

You're no longer dealing with tempting people to click, so you don't care how much your ad looks like an ad. In fact you might even want it to look like an ad, if that's what will keep the advertiser happy.

The most important point to bear in mind here is that you want to make sure that you're not losing money. It might be very nice for the advertiser to have exclusive control over a particular spot on your page but if you can make more money serving CPC (cost per click) ads in that space, then you need to make sure that your site is working for you and not for the advertiser.

Again, watch your stats for a week and see if the revenues you receive for your impressions are higher than those you receive for your clicks.

Most publishers do find that ads that pay by eCPM (earning cost per thousand ads displayed) pay better, especially sites with high traffic rates. After all, you're getting paid for every visitor who comes to your site rather than just those that click, so all you have to do to increase your revenue is increase your traffic. As long as each impression pays more than you're paying for the traffic, you're going to be making a profit. That should be easy to calculate.

If you find the revenues are lower though, then you'll want to boot that ad off and go back to serving conventional ads. You can do that by opting out of showing site-targeted ads (you're automatically opted in).

In general, the biggest problem with these sorts of campaigns is not lower revenues; it's that you've got no idea how long they're going to last, which makes it difficult for you to take advantage of them. If you knew, for example, that you were going to get paid per impression for the next two weeks, then you'd want to buy in as much traffic as possible for that period, provided that you were paying less than you were being paid.

And because you don't care about CTR (clickthrough rate, a percentage generated as a ratio of clicks to ad displays), You could also lay off the optimization and focus on making your site more attractive to users.

But you can't tell when your site is going to be used for a CPM campaign and you can't tell how long it's going to last either. That means there's little point in making major changes to your optimization; you might have to rebuild it the next day.

The best strategy then when you spot a site-targeted ad on your site is to keep a close eye on the cash flows. Buy in more traffic if you can do it profitably but for the most part, just enjoy the extra income!

# CHAPTER
# 3

## Using Colors To Increase Your Clicks

# USING COLORS TO INCREASE YOUR CLICKS

## 3.1 Design Your Website To Highlight AdSense

I once went to a fashion show where each model wore the exact same black outfit for the entire duration of the show.

Boring? Hardly!

The show was intended to showcase platinum jewelry, and the outfits were designed to enhance the jewelry — instead of distracting the audience.

You don't have to make all the pages on your website identical (or black). But you do want to make sure that the look of your page draws attention to the ads — and makes them appear as attractive and as valuable as platinum jewelry.

**Many websites have strong graphic elements that catch the eye — usually at the expense of the AdSense units.**

*If you're using AdSense, be judicious in the selection of fonts, font size, colors, images, tables and other visual aspects of your website.*

**Draw subtle attention to your AdSense units. Make them the stars of your show!**

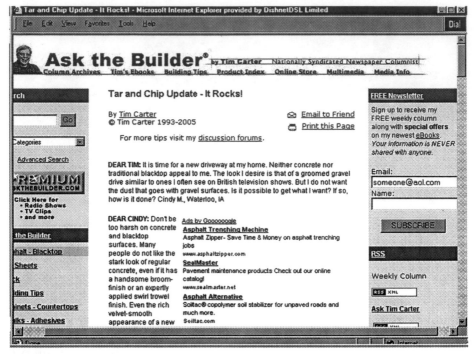

Fig. 3.1   On this website, Tim Carter employs subtle design and placement to make AdSense the center of attraction. Check it out at:

http://www.AskTheBuilder.com

## 3.2  Make The Border Go!

**You can more than DOUBLE your click-through's with this one simple tweak!**

Even before the Internet, ads in newspapers and magazines were marked off with a thick, heavy border. No wonder borders and boxes have come to symbolize advertising messages.

Ads with prominent borders make your pages look cluttered. They distract the eye from the ad text, while marking off the ad blocks from the rest of the content.

*Google provides an extensive color palette in your administrative area (see below). Use it to tweak the look of your ads to suit your web page.*

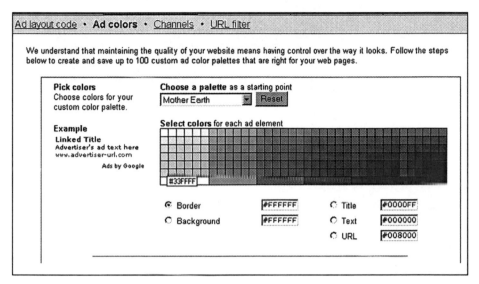

*Fig. 3.2  How to make the border disappear!*

With just one simple click, you can match the color of <u>your ad's border</u> with the background color of <u>your web page</u>. When the border blends with the background, it frees up loads of space. The page looks instantly neater and the ads look more inviting.

Make sure you also pick a matching <u>background color for the ad</u>. The ad's background must match the page background on which the ad will appear.

If the ad appears in a table, match the table background with the ad background.

The key is to blend the background and border color with the page, so that the text looks like an integral part of your web content.

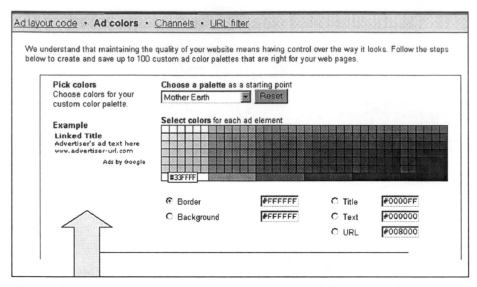

*Fig. 3.3  It's always easier to work with a white background. If your page background is white, you can instantly see the results with the **Example** ad next to the color palette.*

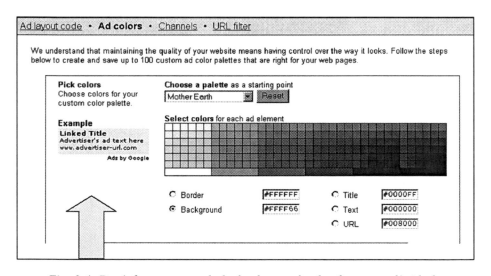

*Fig. 3.4  Don't forget to match the <u>background color for your ad</u> with the background color of <u>your web page</u>. Even with a matching border, the ad in the **Example** above sticks out against the white background.*

**THE ADSENSE CODE**

## 3.3 Text Is Design Too!

That's right: the text size, font, color and the color of your ads must match the other text elements. If the text color of the ads is the same as the text in the body of your page, it'll help the ads blend into the site and make the reader feel that you've endorsed them.

And if the size of the font in the ads is the as the size of the main body of the content, it will have the same effect: they'll look like part of your site and not something brought in by Google.

That's the sort of blending that translates into clicks.

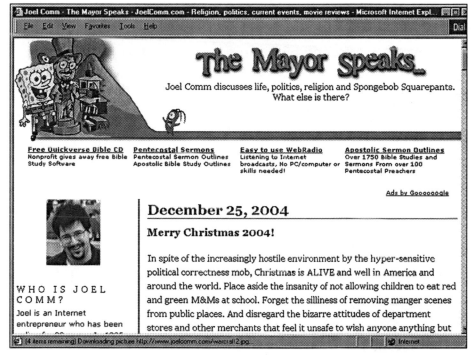

*Fig 3.5 Format your text ads to maximize clicks! On my Blog, I have chosen to use a 728 x 90 leaderboard at the top of my page.*
*See more at http://www.JoelComm.com*

You can see this on my blog. I'm running a test where I've changed the title color of the ads to match the color of the titles on the text. I've also matched the text color of the ads to the color of the site text and the background of the ads to the background of the page.

This **3-way matching** (titles, text and background) can generate excellent click-through rates.

Too many text styles add clutter and can confuse your visitors. Instead, try every legitimate way to make the ads look like a part of your web content.

In other words, use the colors to make sure that your ads **don't look like ads!**

## 3.4  Blue Is Best

So you want to get rid of the border. You want to get your ads the same color as the text on the rest of your page and the background matching the background color of your Web page.

But what about the link itself, the line the user is actually going to click? What color should that be?

That's an easy one: blue.

I used to say that *all* the text in the ad should match the text on your page, including the link. After seeing an article about the benefits of keeping the links blue — and testing extensively — I don't say that any more.

The logic is that users have come to expect links on websites to be blue. Just as they expect stop signs to be red and warning signs to be yellow, so they expect their links to be blue.

**That means people are more likely to click on a blue link than a link in any other color.**

The line in your AdSense code that sets the color of your link is the one that says:

```
Google_color_link = "#color";
```

"#color" is the hexadecimal number for the color you want to use. You should make sure that number is #0000FF.

Keep your link blue and you can experience an increase in click-throughs as high as 25 percent!

## 3.5  Where Did My URL Go?

You can change the color of your text and you can make sure that your links scream, "I'm a FREE road to where you want to go!"

You still have to display the URL. It's one of Google's rules. But you don't have to display it in an obvious manner.

One legitimate trick to make the click-through link less obtrusive is to change the URL display color to match the text description color. Now the link will blend in with the text description and the eye will be drawn to the hyperlink instead of the URL. Google provides these tools for you.  Why not use them?

Note that the 728 x 90 leaderboard and the 468 x 60 banner do not display the URL line by Google's design.  It is not a mistake and you will not get in trouble for the URL not appearing with these ad blocks.  It's just the way it is.

## 3.6  Deliberate Mismatching

When it comes to choosing colors, I recommend 3-way matching and using blue for the links. But there is another strategy that you can use.

You can deliberately mismatch your ad colors and styles, *provided you keep it to the top of your page.*

This distinction generates two powerful 'zones' and therefore two types of experience for the visitor.

The first zone is always at the top of the first page, above the main site banner. The titles and text colors match colors found in the banner graphic heading. (Important — the URL links are hidden, so only certain text ads will allow you to do this.)

The end result is that these ads, placed above the banner graphic look like key control points for your site and are just more likely to be clicked. The visitor feels that they are visiting another major area of that site.

*Fig. 3.6 www.DressesForTheWedding.com has two zones: an ad zone at the top and a free article beneath. Implementing this design increased their revenues FIVE-FOLD!*

# CHAPTER 4

# How To Maximize
# Visibility And Response

# HOW TO MAXIMIZE VISIBILITY AND RESPONSE

## 4.1 Ad Placement: Where To Put Your Ads?

Location is everything. The world's best ad won't deliver if it isn't visible in the first place. But after much experimentation with Google AdSense, I know that the most visible ads aren't always the most effective. In fact, they're likely to get ignored as 'blatant advertising'.

What does work is *wise* placement. Put them where your content is most likely to interest and engage your visitors.

> *You can create several 'points of interest' with the wise use of graphics, tables and other layout techniques.*

Once you have your visitor's attention with engaging and meaningful content, they are most likely to read and click on relevant ads. And that is precisely what Google wants — "educated" clicks from real prospects, not random visits from bored people.

Here are a few simple tips to make your ads 'click'!

## 4.2 Go With The 'Flow'

Identify the reading patterns of your visitors. What draws their attention first? What makes them 'click'?

Like I said, you want to put your ads in areas that draw your visitors in with interesting content. There's no point in putting your ads in some out of the way place where no one ever looks.

Your users will follow your content, so you need to make sure that your ads follow that content too.

Look at the design and layout of your webpage, identify the places that you think most of your users look — and mark each of them as a likely spot to put your ads.

Google actually offers a pretty neat tool to help you identify where your users are most likely to look. Their heat map at *Google.com/support/adsense/bin/static.py?page=tips.html* sums up the options pretty well:

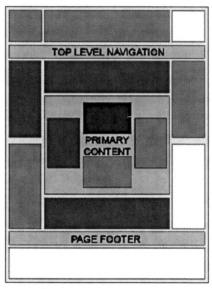

*Fig. 4.1 Google's Heat Map shows an "average" site's hot spots. The darker areas are the regions where people look most frequently. But remember, no site is average. Where do your visitors look most?*

Google says that certain areas are more effective than others. Researchers have also found that when people look at a website, their eyes start in the top left hand corner and then travel down the page from left to right.

All of this is true but the hottest areas can vary from site to site. You will need to experiment to find the very best places for you.

## 4.3 Above The Fold

One general rule on the Internet is that people spend most of their time on a site "above the fold."

The first thing people do when they reach a website is to absorb as much information as possible before they start scrolling. The part of the page that they can see without scrolling is called "above the fold."

That's where you want your ads.

The number of links that appear above the fold affect how likely people are to click on your AdSense ads. That's why more ads doesn't always mean more money! Google always puts the top-paying ads on the top and the lowest-paying ones at the bottom.

If you have a stack with three or more ads, the cheaper ads might steal attention away from high-paying ads and clutter up your website.

You don't want ads and links competing against each other. If you want to increase your earnings per click, remember: Less is More! And that's particularly true above the fold.

Let's take a look at two sample pages:

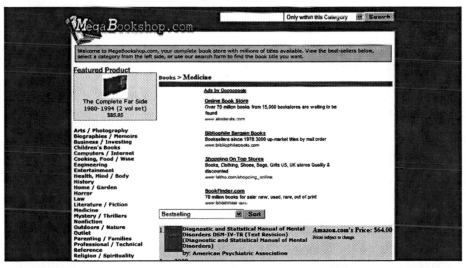

*Fig. 4.2 MegaBookshop.com has a search form, a featured product, category links and AdSense ads, all above the fold.*

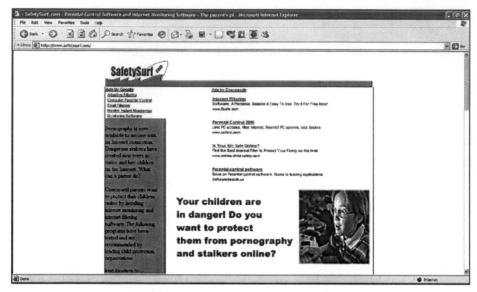

*Fig. 4.3 SafetySurf.com is not the most attractive site, but ONLY*
*has AdSense ads above the fold.*

Now, which of these sites' ads do you think brings a higher click-through rate? You guessed it. The second site has triple the click-through rate of the first site. The moral of the story? If you want to maximize your AdSense clicks, give your visitors fewer choices above the fold!

## 4.4 Using Tables

I've already mentioned that one of the principles of a high click-through rate is to make your sites blend into the page. The more you position your sites to blend into the page, the better your click-through rate will be.

One very neat way to help your ads blend into the site is to place them in tables.

In the example below, Chris Pirillo again skillfully drops his AdSense into a <table> for a clean and attractive look that turns AdSense into a new focal point. See out how he does it at *www.LockerGnome.com*.

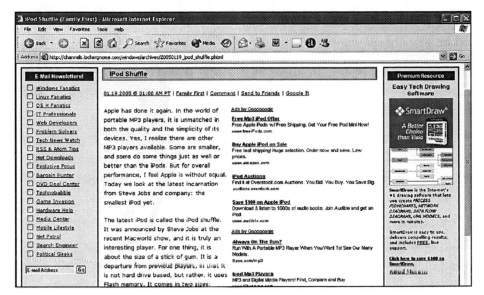

*Fig 4.4 Note how clean the tables make the ads look.*

Want to get the same results with your web page?

Dave Taylor (www.intuitive.com) shares this simple code to create a left or right-aligned table containing AdSense. Just paste this code where you want AdSense to appear.

**Easy!**

Left-aligned table with AdSense:
<table border="0" align="left"><tr><td>
Google AdSense code goes here
</td></tr></table>

Right-aligned table with AdSense:
<table border="0" align="right"><tr><td>
Google AdSense code goes here
</td></tr></table>

## 4.5 Complementing Your Ads

Everything I've discussed so far has been about placing your ads where your users will be looking. That's pretty easy. But there's an alternative strategy, which can be very powerful: bringing your users to your ads.

Now, you have to be careful here. Google forbids you from saying to users "Look over here and click on the ads... I want the money." And that's reasonable. But with some clever design work, you can still guide your users to look in that direction.

The rule to remember here is that **images attract eyes**. When a user loads a Web page, he's always going to look at the pictures. It doesn't matter how interesting the text, how many pictures you've used — or how few — you can be confident that by the time the user clicks away, he'll have looked at all the pictures.

He might not have read all the text, but he will have seen all the pictures.

If you're thinking, "Great, then I'll load up on image ads," think again. There's a difference between seeing the ads and clicking them. Google isn't going to pay you every time a user sees your ad, not even for CPM ads (Google will pay you when the page is loaded, whether the user sees the ad or not.)

Users will see image ads. But they won't click on them.

What you can do though is to place images *near* your ads.

For example, at *SafetySurf.com*, I put a link unit at the top of the page. It's above the side bar, which is where many people put link units, but it's also directly beneath the icon.

People are always going to look at the icon. When they look at the icon, they'll see the ads.

There are all sorts of ways you can do this, but probably the best method is to first place your ads and then think about which images you can place near them.

Of course, you don't just have to use images. You could also use a "Submit" button, a "next" link or anything else that users will have to look at on your page.

A search box for example is an excellent spot. You know your users are about to look for something and click away. Why not offer them some of your own options.

There's a good chance that pulling your users' eyes in this way will increase your click-through rates.

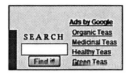

*Fig. 4.5 A new use for a search box at FamilyFirst.com.*

# CHAPTER
# 5

## Controlling
## Your Ads

# CONTROLLING YOUR ADS

## 5.1 Attracting Relevant Ads

Getting the color and placement right will help improve your click-through rate. But neither of those will affect which ads your site serves.

In theory, Google controls the ads that appear on your site. You don't get to choose them at all. In practice, there are a few things that you can do stop irrelevant ads from appearing and ensure that you get the ads that give you cash.

The more relevant the ads, the greater the chance that a user will click and you'll earn money.

The most important factor is obviously going to be your content. Google's crawlers will check your site and serve up ads based on the keywords and the content on your page.

Bear in mind that Google's crawlers can't read graphics or Flash or pretty much anything that isn't text. I'll talk about content in detail in Chapter 9 but for now, remember that if you want to keep your ads relevant, you've got to have the sort of page that Google can understand and use to give you the ads you want.

## 5.2  Keep The Title, Directory And Headlines Relevant

How exactly the crawlers read pages is a secret guarded about as closely as Coca Cola's special syrup formula. One thing that does seem to have an effect though is the title of your URLs and files.

When you create your pages and view them on your computer before uploading them to the server, you should find that AdSense serves up ads related to the name of the directory that holds the page. That gives a pretty big clue as to at least one of the things that Google is looking at: the name of the directory.

Actually, it's not just the name of the directory that's important. The name of the file plays a big part too.

If you have a website about wedding trains and the title of one of your pages is trains.php for example, there's a good chance that you'll get ads about Amtrak and Caltrain. That wouldn't give you many clicks. Change the name of the file to weddingtrains.php and there's a much better chance that you'll see ads related to weddings.

If you find that the ads that are appearing on your site have nothing to do with your content, the first places to look are your directory and your title. Make them more relevant to your content and you should find that you get better ads.

Another place to look is your headlines. Instead of using a <font> tag for your heading, try using the <h1> tag with headings that contain your keywords. That should help them to stand out to the crawlers.

And if you don't have any headlines at all, try adding some.

## 5.3 Finding Keywords

We know that Google's crawlers searches websites for keywords, then reports back and tells the company what kind of ads to send to the site. If your site is about pension plans for example, then your keywords would be things like "retirement", "401k" and "pension".

Getting the right keywords on your site won't just make your ads relevant; it will also help you to make sure that the ads you get are the ones that pay the most.

There are all sorts of tools available on the Web that tell you how much people are prepared to pay for keywords. *www.Overture.com* and *www.Googlest.com* let you see how much people are prepared to pay, and *Keywords.ClickHereForIt.com* also has a list of keywords with their prices.

Again, you don't want to build a site just to cash in on a high paying keyword but if you know that "401k" pays more than "retirement" for example, then it makes sense to use the higher paying keywords more than the lower paying ones.

See chapter 15 for more on finding the most up-to-date high paying keywords.

## 5.4 Keyword Density

You'll need the right keywords to get the right ads. But you'll also need the right amount of keywords.

There's no golden rule for the putting right number of keywords on a page to get the ads you want. You'll just have to experiment. It also seems to be the case that keyword density is counted across pages, especially for high-paying keywords. If you have a site that's generally about cars and you write a page for car rental, a higher-paying keyword, you might find that you need to produce several pages about car rental before you get the ads.

In general though, if you find that your ads are missing the point of your page and that your titles are all correct, then the next step would be to try mentioning your keywords more often and make sure that they're all finely focused. For example, talking about "fire extinguishers" is likely to get you better results than talking generally about "safety equipment."

## 5.5 Keyword Placement

It shouldn't really matter where you put your keywords, should it? As long as the right words are on the right page in the right amount of numbers, that should be enough to get you relevant ads, right?

Wrong.

One of the strangest results that people have had using AdSense is that putting keywords in particular places on the page can have an effect on the ads the site gets.

**The most important place on your webpage is directly beneath the AdSense box.** The keywords you place there could influence your ads.

For example, mentioning clowns in the space directly beneath the AdSense box could give you ads about circuses and red noses!

Keeping that in mind, you could play with your ads in all sorts of ways. If you had a site about camping for example, you might find that you're getting lots of ads about tents and sleeping bags, which would be fine. But if you also wanted to make sure that one or two of your ads were about Yosemite or mobile homes, then mentioning those keywords once or twice on the page directly below the AdSense box could give you ads for sites with that sort of content too.

Bear in mind though that you'll often find that you get ads that try to combine the main thrust of your site with the words in that keyword space below the ad box. So if you had a site about gardening and you mentioned "cabbages" beneath the ad box, you're more likely to get ads about growing cabbages than ads about cabbage recipes.

Experimenting with the placement of the keywords could allow you to control at least one or two of the ads you receive and help keep them varied. That's definitely something to try.

## 5.6  Keyword Frames

One of the reasons that websites don't always receive relevant ads may be that all the navigation and other non-content words affect the way Google reads the page. If your links and other words take up lots of space, it could well skew your results.

One way to avoid your navigation affecting your ads is simply to create frames. You put all of your content in your main frame and the navigation material in a separate frame. Only the "content frame" has the Google code (google_page_url = document.location), so your keywords won't be diluted by non-relevant words.

## 5.7 Section Targeting

Probably the most effective way to ensure the crawlers read the keywords you want to emphasize though is to use Section Targeting. This is a fantastic technique. By simply inserting a couple of lines of HTML code into your Web page, you can tell the crawler which parts of your site are the most important and ensure that you get ads relevant to that content.

The lines you want to use to emphasize particular sections of your Web page are:

<!— google_ad_section_start —>

*Section text.*

<!— google_ad_section_end —>

The rest of the page won't be ignored, but those particular lines will receive a heavier weighting. If you want to tell the crawlers to ignore particular sections, you can use these lines:

<!— google_ad_section_start(weight=ignore) —>

*Section text.*

<!— google_ad_section_end —>

You can highlight (and de-emphasize) as many or as few sections as you wish, but what you can't do is use these instructions solely to highlight keywords. So you can't put them around particular single words or phrases on your page and hope to see ads that relate only to those terms.

In fact, Google recommends that you highlight a sizeable portion of text — as much as 20 percent — for the targeting to be most effective. The result of targeting small amounts of text could be irrelevant ads, public service ads... or even a banning if you deliberately tried to bring up ads that have nothing to do with your site.

Section Targeting is probably most useful if you have a Web page that covers lots of different topics. So if you had a blog about MP3 players but had written an article about rap music for example, you could use Section Targeting to ensure that you didn't lose ads about the music players to ads about rap music. Or you could tell the crawlers to ignore your readers' comments and focus on your own entries.

And presumably, there's nothing wrong with stuffing a paragraph with keywords related to your subject and telling the crawlers to focus on that section to ensure that your ads stay targeted.

It's definitely something that you want to play with.

If there's one problem with Section Targeting though, it's that it can take up to two weeks before you see the results — the time it can take for the crawler to re-visit your page. So it's not a fast process and that can make it a bit of a blunt tool. But it's not blunt enough to be ignored.

## 5.8 No 'Baiting'!

Often I've clicked through a 'promising' website, only to find reams of keyword spam, interspersed with AdSense. Websites like these make AdSense look bad.

Keyword spam may trick search spiders, but your human visitors will leave disappointed.

**People hate being 'baited' by a web marketer**. Offer content that makes their visit worthwhile. **Address the needs and concerns of your visitors with original content**.

Quality content builds trust and loyalty — and that, in turn, makes people want to click. Search rankings may change, but loyal visitors keep coming back for more!

## 5.9  Changing Metatags

Metatags certainly aren't what they used to be, and in AdSense they're barely anything at all. There's a good chance that when it comes to deciding ad relevance, your metatags have no effect whatsoever.

I've already mentioned that the title of your page will have an effect. It's also very likely that the description does too.

But that doesn't mean that your metatags are completely irrelevant when it comes to AdSense. They aren't. They're only seem to be irrelevant when it comes to serving ads; they still play a role in search engine optimization and getting your site indexed faster.

## 5.10  Inviting The Robot

So far in this chapter, I've explained some of the ways that you can tweak your page to keep your ads relevant. But the changes you make won't have any effect until Google's robot stops by and re-indexes your page. What will generally happen is that once you upload your new page, you'll still get the old ads and you might have to wait some time before the robot visits it again and you can find out whether your changes have the right result.

To get the robot to stop by earlier, reload the page in your browser, and then again a few minutes later. Do not click on any of the ads just reload and wait a few minutes before attempts.

This doesn't always work but with a bit of luck, you should find that you receive new ads within a few minutes.

## 5.11  Public Service Ads

The penalty for not getting your keyword placement and density right isn't just irrelevant ads. It could also be no ads at all. If Google can't find any relevant ads to give you, it could use your space to present public service ads, which are very nice but they don't pay you a penny.

You might prefer to earn money and give it to a charity of your choice rather than give space on your site to a cause that Google chooses.

The most obvious way to beat this problem is to specify an alternate URL in the event that Google has no ads for you. You can do this from your AdSense account. Instead of linking to the Red Cross or whoever it may be, you'll receive a link to a site that you've pre-chosen. For example, I have set up default ads for my 336 x 280 ad block, placed them at *www.WorldVillage.com/336x280-1.html* and chosen them as my URL.

*Fig. 5.1 My own version of AdSense.*

They look remarkably like AdSense ads, don't you think?

You can also use this space to deliver image-based ads that come from your server. For offers that pay per action (clicks or signups), I like to use *WebSponsors.com*. You can signup for a free account and find new ways to monetize your unused ad space.

Or can try Google Backfill, a very neat service that allows you to select keywords relevant to your site and display targeted ads instead of the public service ads or your alternative URL. They'll match your colors and styles and split the revenue 50/50. It's all in line with Google's TOS and makes good alternative to no revenue at all while you get your keywords fixed. The service is available at *www.AllFeeds.com*.

Probably the easiest way to turn that wasted space into revenue though is to use GoogleAdSensePlus. This is another very neat tool that lets you swap public service ads for ads to a URL of your choice or your product. They have video online that you can watch to see how it works.

It's really very simple and very effective.

## 5.12 Blocking Ads

Another useful way to control the ads you see on your site is to block ads you don't want.

Google gives you a limit of 200 URLs to block, which isn't much. You might well find yourself burning through them pretty fast, especially if you try to block lower paying ads in favor of the higher-paying ones.

Playing with keywords, content and placement will give you much better results.

## 5.13 "Advertise On This Site"

Finally, there is one more way to influence the ads that you show on your site through AdSense: by keeping active the "Advertise on this site" feature. (You begin an AdSense campaign opted in; you have to choose to opt out.)

The feature displays a small notice beneath the ads that potential advertisers can click to sign up for AdWords. You don't get paid when the advertiser clicks but if they do sign up, their ads will appear on your page on a pay-per-impression basis, provided the price they enter beats other bids.

While you can't choose which advertisers will sign up — or even see which advertisers are signing up — you can be reasonably confident that any advertiser looking at your site and choosing to advertise on it is likely to be in a relevant field. You can also use the filters to block advertisers that you don't want to promote.

There are two things to consider when inviting people to advertise on your site.

First, if there's one message I've been trying to push throughout this book, it's that you don't want to make your ads look like ads. Keep your "Advertise on this site" feature switched on and you're going to get the word "Advertise" right next to an ad that you've just spent hours trying to blend into your site.

That's not the sort of thing that's going to make an ad look like content.

| ContentKeeper - WebFilter | Advanced Web Filter |
|---|---|
| Monitor, Manage and Control Staff Internet Access | Free 14 day trial. Block websites by name or type - Kid Safe Internet |
| Ads by Goooooogle | Advertise on this site |

*Fig. 5.2 Emphasizing your ads with "Advertise on this site."*

Sure, you've also got "Ads by Google" right next to it but you want to de-emphasize your ads as much as possible, not push the fact that they came from a third party.

What effect will that little notice have on your click-through rate? That's something you'll need to check. Once you've optimized your ads, opt out of the "Advertise on this site" feature for a week and check your CTR. Then opt back in and compare the results.

That should let you know how much you're paying for the chance of receiving a targeted CPM campaign.

When you do get targeted in that way, you can then see how much the campaign brings in and decide whether or not the lower CTR is worth the expense.

On the whole, I think that for sites with plenty of traffic and who can earn large sums from a CPM campaign, it's usually worthwhile staying in; other sites will need to do some careful calculations but most will also find that the lost clicks are minimal and that opting in pays.

It can pay even more when you consider the second issue related to "Advertise on this site": **you can edit the landing page**.

When an advertiser clicks on that advertising link, they're going to pull up a page on Google with information about AdSense — and about your site. Google sees this page as a co-brand: they host and supply it, you can do what you like with it. Advertisers that don't yet have an AdWords account will be shown how to sign up and place their ads on your pages, and advertisers that do have an account will be shown how to advertise on your site.

Google lets you make three kinds of changes to this page:

- You can add a logo;
- You can set the color scheme;
- And you can write your own welcome message.

Do you see why these options are so important?

*This is the only place in AdSense where publishers get to talk directly to advertisers.*

That's crucial!

AdSense is structured so that Google stands between the network of advertisers and the network of publishers. Ads go in one end, Google sorts them and sends them out the other end.

Advertisers have no way of telling publishers to put their ads at the top of the page or next to relevant pictures or only on pages that contain positive reviews of their products, or anything else. Once they've submitted their ads, they just have to trust the publisher to promote their sites in the best way possible.

Similarly, as publishers, we have no control over what advertisers write in their ads. We can't tell them to use particular keywords, to write certain things in their headlines or to produce their copy in a particular style.

If we get an ad with bad copy, we just have to put up with the lower CTR until we either block it or see it replaced by a more profitable ad.

Edit the landing page, and *you can tell the advertisers what they should write to get the most clicks with an ad on your site.*

**You can even include your email address and contact information and invite them to contact you directly.**

*Fig. 5.3 The "Advertise on this site" landing page, your communication channel to advertisers.*

You want that page to look like part of your site. If an advertiser has clicked on the "Advertise" link on your site, it's because they've liked what they've seen. You've impressed them, not Google, not Google's robot and not Google's method of matching ads to publishers.

Google understands that means they've got more chance of signing up an advertiser if they let *you* do the selling.

You should certainly add your logo to this page. It appears in the top left-hand corner and makes the landing page look like you've endorsed it — which, of course, you have. If you don't have a logo, this is a good time to create one. You could just use any graphic that appears on your site; the effect will still be to draw a link between the landing page and your site.

And that's the effect you want.

At the moment, you only get one landing page per account, although that might change soon. If you have multiple sites, Google will make sure that the ads only appear on the site the advertiser was visiting when he clicked, but you might not want to mention a site name on the landing page in case you confuse the advertiser.

The color scheme, of course, should match the colors used on your site.

It's in the welcome text that things can really get interesting.

You don't really want to give advertisers a list of keywords that they should use. It's unlikely that they're going to be impressed by a bunch of demands from someone who has yet to earn them a dime.

But they will appreciate information about the sorts of words that are likely to attract the most clicks. They'll still feel that they've got the freedom to decide on their own ad copy — but they'll be more likely to write the sort of copy you want.

For example, if you have a site about cars and you know your users are particularly interested in models that suit families, you could let the advertisers know. If your blog mostly attracts Republicans you could suggest issues that are likely to get your users clicking an ad. If you've got a site about pets, you could point out that your users are more interested in accessories for dogs than for cats.

No one knows your users better than you. This is the place to share that information so that you can share some higher revenues.

And finally, you could also encourage advertisers to sign up for a targeted-site campaign.

While it's likely that most of the advertisers who click on the link will want to advertise exclusively on your site — and Google has set up the system to encourage that result — it's also possible that some advertisers who are new to AdSense will decide to spread their ads over a number of different sites in your field.

That means you're only getting a fraction of their advertising budget. A targeted-site campaign will give you all of it.

Just tell them that a targeted campaign on your site is likely to give them the best results.

Does all that sound hard? Don't worry, I'll make it easy for you. You can just take the text below and adjust it for your site, swapping the underlined sections for details relevant to your site:

> Thank you for advertising on <u>FamilyFirst.com</u>, the web's leading site for <u>family-friendly web site reviews</u>. Our users are typically <u>traditional families, stay-at-home moms</u> and <u>parents of children aged between 3 and 16</u>.
>
> We've found that users respond most favorably to articles and links about <u>filter software</u>, <u>children's DVDs and computer games</u>, <u>toys</u> and <u>family entertainment</u>.
>
> Highlighting these aspects of your business in your ad is likely to earn the highest number of clicks and the best conversions.
>
> We'd also recommend that you focus your advertising with a targeted-site campaign. We look forward to helping your business grow! If you would like more information about advertising on <u>FamilyFirst.com</u>, please write to <u>Sales@FamilyFirst.com</u>.

See how easy that is?

The page should be available within 24 hours, and once you've created it, you can put links to it anywhere you like; you're not restricted to the little line under the ads. So you could put them in your emails and on your Web pages in places of your choice.

Why would you send potential advertisers to Google's advertising sign-up page instead of your own? Well, you might not want to. You might prefer to just vet each advertiser yourself and set your own price. But bear in mind that any advertiser who follows that link has to outbid other advertisers on Google who want that same space. You don't know what exactly the current highest bid is; the most you can know is how many clicks your ads received and how much money you earned in the previous days and weeks.

You certainly can't tell how much you're *going* to receive in the weeks to come.

Sending potential advertisers to your Google sign-in page will ensure that you're always getting the highest-paying ads for those spaces.

## 5.14 Does Location Matter For CPM Ads?

In a word, yes! This is what Google has to say about CPM ads, the type of ads you're like to get from a site-targeted campaign (my emphasis):

> *You'll earn revenue each time a CPM (cost per 1000 impressions, also known as **pay-per-impression**) ad is displayed on your site. You won't earn additional revenue for clicks on these ads.*
>
> ***Please note that the placement of CPM ads on your pages can affect the amount an advertiser pays for that impression.** Placing your CPM ad units **below the fold**, or in an otherwise **low-impact location**, may result in **lower earnings than if the ad unit was placed in a conspicuous location**.*

So if you were thinking, "Great! I'll encourage click-throughs above the fold and get paid per impression with an expanded text ad at the bottom of the page..." think again.

Google claims that CPM campaigns have to bid for space on publishers' websites in the same marketplace as CPC ads, and that therefore you would only receive a CPM ad if it's the highest paying option. If advertisers are paying less for a CPM ad at the bottom of a page, it's less likely that you're going to get one down there.

Now, how Google is figuring out where on the page you're putting your ads beats me. Their love of Smart Pricing (see Chapter 11) though, suggests that they could be comparing advertisers' sales results with the number of impressions and assuming that sites with high impressions and low sales have put the ads in out-of-the-way places.

Whichever method they're using, the end result is that you're still going to see higher revenues from ads in the best locations and less from the worst spots.

# CHAPTER
# 6

# Catch Fickle Visitors
# With The Google
# Search Box

# CATCH FICKLE VISITORS WITH THE GOOGLE SEARCH BOX

## 6.1 Finding Money With Search

What happens when your visitors can't find what they want on your website? They might be bored, probably they're hungry for more or they might want to refine their search. If you have a Google Search Box, you can now retain these 'quitters' — and make money from ads they click from their search results!

The Google Search Box isn't just an added convenience for your visitors — it can actually make you money!

If your AdSense ads are being ignored, add a link at the bottom of the AdSense ads, inviting visitors to try Google search. A simple note should do the trick. Try something like: "Can't find what you're looking for? Try Google Search!"

A Google Search box allows your visitors to specify their exact search terms, thereby "pulling" more relevant ads to your page. Using the Search feature, you can pull up **on-demand AdSense ads** at the top of the search results.

> *At the bottom of the Google text ads, place a link to the Google Search bar, inviting readers to Search for better-targeted content and offers. When visitors click an ad, YOU get paid!*

*You can invite users to search within the website or the entire web. As far as possible, **use a staid gray button for the Google search feature**. It looks more believable — and legitimate! Note that Google has not played around with its own search buttons, although the logo itself has undergone many theme-based transformations.*

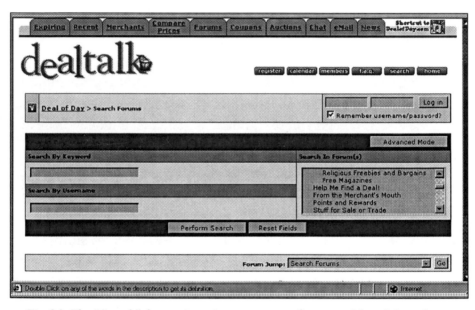

*Fig 6.1 The "Search" feature is an important part of content-rich websites. On my website above, users are invited to search different threads within the website 'by keyword' and 'by username'. Check it out at: http://Forums.DealOfDay.com/search.php?*

Google Search Boxes are getting increasingly popular with Internet Forums, enabling users to pull up relevant text ads "on demand"!

## 6.2 Learn How To Add Google Search To Your Web Page

Adding Google Search to your Web page is very easy. This step-by-step tutorial shows you how:

**1.** Log in to your AdSense Account and click the "**Account Information**" tab.

**2.** From the **Account Information** Page, click on "**Products**" and then the "**Edit Information**" button to Subscribe to **AdSense for Search.**

**3.** Click the "**Search Settings**" tab to specify your search preferences and results. Paste the html code on your web page and start turning those clicks into AdSense cash!

## 6.3 To Search Or Not To Search

Putting a Google search box on your site brings advantages and disadvantages. The big plus is that all the ads the user sees are going to be relevant. The user chooses the keyword so the results are going to be right in line with what the user wants.

On the other hand, that means you've got no control over the keywords they choose so you can't try to promote high-paying keywords. You have to take what you're given. You could have a high click-through rate but low revenues (although there's still no guarantee that the user will click on an ad rather than an unpaid listing on the search results page.)

But your users will leave your site at some point anyway. Why shouldn't you try to make money when they do click away? Even if Search doesn't bring you huge amounts of money, you should still use it as an added revenue source and to bring extra functionality to your users.

I look at it this way. If a visitor doesn't find what they want on my site, I'd prefer that they leave some change in the "tip jar" on the way out the door!

## 6.4 Home Page Searching

One way to increase your revenues from searching is to encourage your users to use your site as their home page.

Many users have Google as their home page. If you're offering the same service as Google, using their search box and delivering their results, there's no reason why they shouldn't be searching from your page — and giving you revenue from the ads.

Just encourage your users, especially users with Google as their home page, to switch to you, and you'll be able to make the most of your search function and your ads.

## 6.5 Customizing Your Search

Google lets you customize the search box to match your site in the same way that you can customize your ad units. But a different principle applies here: you want to prevent your ads from looking like ads; you want your search box to look like a search box.

You can certainly make the box look like part of your site so that it looks attractive but as I said, keep the button grey.

People trust Google to deliver results that they want. If the search box reminds them of Google, they're more likely to use it than go to Google.com and search from there.

# CHAPTER
# 7

# AdSense And Firefox
# Referral Programs

# ADSENSE AND FIREFOX REFERRAL PROGRAMS

So we've talked about text ads, image ads, link units and search boxes. There is one more way of making money with AdSense: referral programs.

Referral programs work in a similar way to the other AdSense advertising programs but with some important differences. First, the prices are fixed. There is no bidding process for the referral program. Before you sign up, you'll know exactly what you're likely to earn when a user clicks.

The ad also stays exactly the same. While you can choose from a selection of different image ads (and at the moment, there are only image ads available although there are hints of text links to come), you won't have to wonder which ads are going to be served or how you can play around with the keywords to bring up the ads you want.

What you see on the ad format page of the referral program in your AdSense account is what you get.

Google is currently two referral programs: one to promote AdSense, and one to promote the Firefox Web browser.

## 7.1 Referring For AdSense

On the face of it, of the two referral programs, the AdSense program looks the most lucrative. It pays $100 each time a sign-up earns $100 in revenue. If ten of your users click, sign up for AdSense and earn $100, you'll have made an easy thousand dollars.

The product is good, the company is sound and the referral buttons are very attractive. In fact, they look like they were inspired by the iPod and that's been eye-catching enough!

In practice though, few publishers have reported massive incomes using this referral program. That might be because it's still early and sign-ups have yet to break through the $100 barrier. (Without the right techniques, that can take a while; with the right techniques, it can happen very quickly indeed.)

But it might also be because AdSense is just so popular there are precious few serious publishers around who aren't already using it. You can only hope to catch those people who are coming online now.

And of course, you'd expect to see a much lower CTR for an AdSense referral ad than for your traditional text ads; these ads aren't contextualized.

If you've got a site selling pet food or a blog about life as high school teacher, only a tiny fraction of your visitors are going to have a website. Only a tiny fraction of those people are going to click.

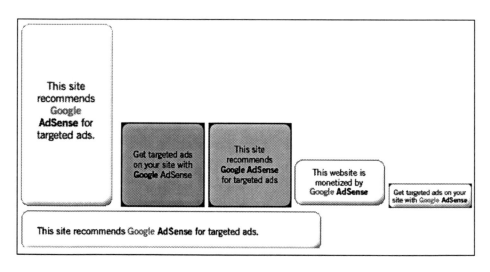

*Fig. 7.1 AdSense referral buttons come in different shapes and sizes... and some look like iPods. (Images not to scale.)*

And not all of those will generate $100 any time soon.

It's also worth remembering that you can't format these buttons in any way at all. The most you can do is play with the placement. (Although you can state on your site that you recommend AdSense and Firefox, even if you can't ask your users specifically to click.)

But I'd still recommend that when it comes to placement, you give top priority to your text ads.

These sorts of buttons are going to stand out anywhere on the page. They're always going to look like ads and people will see them and recognize them wherever they are.

The best strategy for these buttons is first to allocate places to your other AdSense ads. You can then toss in a button in whatever space you've got left on the page.

Sound brutal?

Maybe it is. But financially it makes sense.

You might bring in a few extra bucks with an AdSense referral button but it would just be the cherry on the cake. Your AdSense ads are your cake, so focus on that.

## 7.2 Firing Up Firefox

The same is true of your Firefox referral ads. These pay $1 for every user who downloads the Firefox Web browser with an attached Google toolbar.

Again, they can't be formatted or changed, so you can only play with placement. But at least you know exactly how much money you're going to receive when someone downloads:

One dollar.

And that's when the user downloads, not when he clicks.

You've probably noticed that I'm not exactly rushing out to put a down payment on a private Caribbean island at the thought of these referral buttons.

I just haven't found that they're going to bring in a great deal of extra revenue, and I'm not aware of any other publisher who's managed to prove me wrong.

That doesn't mean I'm not going to use them. An extra buck here or there isn't going to do me any harm. And if you'd like to see people moving away from Internet Explorer, then being paid to do it can't be bad.

(Although if you compare the amount that Google are paying for these buttons with the amount you can earn with similar ads from other companies, then you might be even less enthusiastic; they don't compare well.)

Like the AdSense referral buttons, you should only think of the Firefox referral buttons as a little bit of extra revenue... and enjoy it!

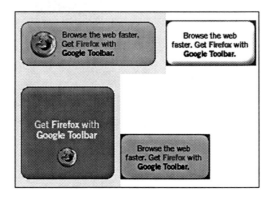

*Fig. 7.2 Firefox referral buttons. Pretty but not very lucrative.*

# CHAPTER
# 8

## Using Multiple
## Ad Blocks

# USING MULTIPLE AD BLOCKS

Google lets you place more than one ad unit on each page of your Web site. In fact, you can place:

*3 ad units*

*2 AdSense for search boxes*

*1 link unit*

*1 AdSense referral button*

*1 Firefox referral button*

What does this mean for web publishers?

A real bonanza: you now have many more chances to hook readers with new ads as Google will show unique ads in each ad unit!

With multiple ad blocks, you can also decide which ads are served in the best places for your site.

## 8.1 How Many Ads Is Too Many?

In general, I recommend that you put as many AdSense units on your page as possible. The more choices you give your users, the more likely they are to click.

The only caveat to this is ad-blindness. Put lots of ads on your site and users are just going to ignore them. And when they ignore one unit, they're likely to ignore them all.

This can be more of a problem for small Web pages than for larger pages such as those on blogs. On a short page, all those different ads can quickly outweigh the content; on a long page, you can scatter them about so that they're less likely to get in the way of a user's reading.

One great solution is to have a long home page with lots of ads but which contains only the headlines and the first paragraph or so from each article. To read more, the user has to click to a page with just that one article.

That page would have fewer units. But because those units would be influenced by just one article, the ads would be better targeted.

## 8.2 What To Do With Three Ad Units

The actual number of ads that you'll choose will depend on the design of your site. But considering the range of different formats, you should find it pretty easy to squeeze in at least two ad units and usually three.

Most sites for example, have room for a leaderboard (although you should also experiment with a link unit to see which of the two in that position gives you the best results).

It's also not too difficult to insert a rectangular unit into an article. You can do that with just about any article.

That's two units already.

The final unit, a button or vertical banner, could do very well in a sidebar.

Most people choose to keep the ads far apart, but you can also have some pretty dramatic effects by putting your ad units together. This isn't a strategy that's going to work for everyone, but creating a zone — at the top of your page maybe or between blog entries — can really make those ads look like content.

After all, users are used to seeing ads in single blocks. When they see a whole section of the page given over to ads, there's a good chance they'll assume it's content and give it some extra attention.

## 8.3 Where To Put The Search Boxes

The search boxes are usually easier. Probably the most popular place for these is one of the top corners or in the side bar.

You could try putting the second one at the bottom of the page if you want to give users somewhere to go when they've finished reading, but to be frank, I doubt if you'll make any more money with a search box down there than you would from the one at the top.

They're a good way to capture revenue from users who don't click on the ads and are about to leave, but I don't think that putting two search boxes on a page is going to give you more income than one. It's possible and you can try it. But I wouldn't expect any massive results.

## 8.4 Google Is Mean With The Link Units

Two search boxes might not make much of a difference, but I think that two link units might. They're small enough to squeeze into all sorts of spots and they look so good at the top and bottom of a list of links that you could probably have fun with three or four of them.

You've got one.

Fortunately, you can put it just about anywhere. Because the link unit looks very different to an ad unit, I don't think you have to worry too much about them competing for clicks — and ending up with nothing. They go very well with other ad units.

## 8.5 Put Referral Buttons Near Ad Units

I think that the referral buttons are most eye-catching when kept together. That might mean you get fewer clicks on them — one button looks like a special offer; two looks like a pair of ads — but who cares?

You'll make more money with your ad units than with your referral buttons.

Put a pair of referral buttons next to an ad unit and you'll draw your user's eyes in that direction. The products aren't interesting enough for most users to click; the incomes aren't high enough for you to care a great deal if they don't; but where the buttons are really strong is in the design.

You can double that power and draw on it by putting the buttons together and placing them near the ads that really can make money.

## 8.6 Putting It All Together

Deciding where to put one ad can often be difficult. There are so many different options. Get it wrong and it will cost you money.

While having multiple ads lets you tempt users wherever they are on the page, it also compounds the problem. What's the best combination of ads and where should the different ads go?

Experimentation and close tracking is the only real way to know for your site but you have to start somewhere. I've put three suggested starting points below. These aren't meant to be final versions that will yield you the greatest income. They're just meant to get you started quickly. You can then try swapping the locations of different units and see how those changes affect your CTR.

## 8.7 Putting Multiple Ads In Articles

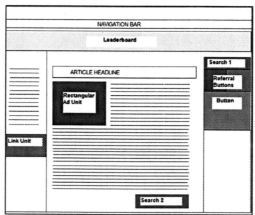

*Fig. 8.1 Distributing multiple ads on an article Web page.*

On a Web page that features just one article, you could place a leaderboard beneath the navigation bar, a rectangular ad unit embedded at the beginning of the article and a link unit in a list of links in the left-hand sidebar.

On the right, you could place a search box and a couple of referral buttons to draw attention to a third ad unit located above another set of links, perhaps to archives, news or anything else. You could also try a second search box at the bottom of the page.

Possible alternatives to try:

- Swapping the leaderboard for a link unit
- Replacing the link unit on the left with a vertical banner
- Placing a half-banner at the end of the article instead of the second search box
- Moving the link unit on the left to the top of the sidebar
- Using a skyscraper on the right instead of a button
- Or just taking out some of the ads to see if that brings in more clicks

## 8.8 Putting Multiple Ads In Blogs

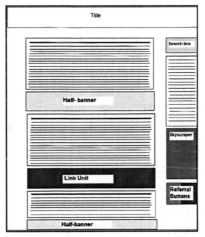

*Fig. 8.2 Distributing multiple ads on a blog.*

The best places to put ads on a blog is between the blog entries. Link units would probably be ideal here... but you've only got one of them. Instead, you could start with a half-banner or even a full banner and use a link unit in between two of the blog entries.

A search button can be placed at the top of a sidebar on the right with a skyscraper blended into a list of links, and the referral buttons at the bottom.

Possible alternatives to try:

- Swapping the link unit for another ad unit and using a link unit in place of the skyscraper

- Using banners instead of half-banners

- Embedding a rectangular ad unit into the text of the blog

- Placing ad units next to photos in the blogs

- Adding an extra search box to the bottom of the right-hand sidebar

## 8.9 Putting Multiple Ads In Merchant Sites

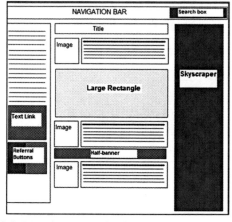

*Fig. 8.3 Distributing multiple ads on a merchant site.*

There are really two approaches you can take to using AdSense on merchant sites. The first is simply to treat them in the same way as blogs:

put a link at the end of each section of advertising copy and place a banner or half banner beneath it. That ad unit should blend into the text above and below. You can use a skyscraper on the edge of the screen, a link unit beneath a list of navigation links, a search box at the top of the page and referral buttons wherever they can make the page look good.

Alternatively, you could use the images of your products to draw attention to your ads by placing small units near them, either directly beneath the pictures or right next to them.

In the sample layout above, I've placed a large rectangular ad unit directly beneath a featured product. The feature would create the most attention and users would have read past it to reach the rest of the page.

Whenever you're using AdSense on merchant sites though do keep a close eye on the ads you're serving; you don't want to advertise your competitors!

Possible alternatives to try:

- Using a text link instead one of the ad units between the marketing copy
- Placing a large picture of a product on a page... and an ad unit right next to it
- Using banners instead of half-banners
- Placing a leaderboard either at the top of the page or at the bottom
- Separating each piece of marketing copy with a large square unit

And if you're worried you've put in too many ad units... just take one out and see if your CTR changes.

# CHAPTER
# 9

## Building Content

# BUILDING CONTENT

## 9.1 Writing Content

AdSense works better than just about every other type of online advertising for one simple reason: the ads are relevant to the content on your page. Users click on the ads because they find them interesting.

And they come back and click on them again because they find your content interesting.

If your site doesn't have good content, you're going to struggle to attract users and links, and you won't be able to persuade anyone to come back to your site.

Having the right content then is crucial to having good revenues with AdSense. It's also crucial to the relationship you have with Google's indexing mechanism. Remember, Google is a search engine first and foremost. Their purpose is to provide the web user with the best search results for the terms they are seeking. If you are providing quality content, you have a greater chance of seeing your search results come up higher on the page.

Fortunately, it's also easier than ever to fill your site with page after page of sticky content, each of which contains ad units and opportunities to earn revenue.

The most obvious way to create content is of course to **write it yourself**. Pick a subject you like and pour your heart out.

If you know everything there is to know about video games, you could set up a site stuffed with reviews, news and walkthroughs, and write all the articles yourself. Your AdSense units will give you ads related to gaming and as long as they're positioned properly and look right they should give you more than enough revenue to fund your video gaming habit and then some. You can do the same thing for any topic you wanted.

But remember, if you've created your site to make money, then writing the content yourself means that you're *working* for that money. When you count your revenues, you have to factor in the time and effort it took you to make those revenues.

That's one of the reasons that many people look for other, easier ways to get content around their ads. (The fact that they just don't like writing is another good reason.) Fortunately, there's plenty of ways of creating effortless content and some of them are even free.

## 9.2 Making Bucks With Blogs

Writing blogs isn't exactly effortless, but it is something a lot of people do for fun and because they're updated regularly, Google loves them. If you're going to write a blog anyway, then you should certainly be making money out of it.

The biggest challenge when writing a blog is getting ads that give you good revenues. Because your entries are going to be talking about all sorts of different things, there's a chance that you're going to get ads on all sorts of random topics.

That's fine, unless your ads are barely giving you enough revenue to pay for the blog.

If you find that you're getting lots of ads related to "blogs" for example, instead of what you're blogging about, you can try changing the meta name in your template. Delete the <$Metainfodata$> tag and replace it with your own keywords and description:

<meta name="robots" content="index,follow">

<meta name="keywords" Content="Your keywords">

<meta name="description" Content="Keyword-rich description">

Make sure that your blog has plenty of keywords and use lots of headlines containing key phrases, repeating them throughout the blog.

Above all though, make sure that your blog has plenty of text. It might be fun to stuff your pages with pictures of friends, family and pets but Google can't read them and you'll end up with public service ads instead of revenue.

## 9.3 Adding AdSense To Your Blog

Not all blog sites use the same template so how you add AdSense to your blog will depend on the company you're using.

For users of Blogspot.com, which is owned by Google, you can put the ads in the template section of the site:

```
<!— Begin .post —>

<div class="post"><a name="<$BlogItemNumber$>"></a>

<BlogItemTitle>

<h3 class="post-title">

<BlogItemUrl><a  href="<$BlogItemUrl$>"  title="external link"></BlogItemUrl>

<.$BlogItemTitle$>

<BlogItemUrl></a></BlogItemUrl>

</h3>

</BlogItemTitle>

<!—Your AdSense code —>
```

You can see on my own blog at *www.JoelComm.com* how I put ads directly above my text. *Crayfish-Info.BlogSpot.com* does the same. The ads here are centered above the <div> tag and he's added a <br> break tag to add a gap between the head and Google and help his ads to stand out.

To do the same thing to your Blogspot blog, click "Change Settings" on the Dashboard and then click "Template Tab." Somewhere on the page, below the CSS material, you should find a section of code that begins"

```
<p id="description"><$BlogDescription$></p>

</div></div><br>
```

The code should then look like this:

```
<div align="center">

<script type="text/javascript"><!—

google_ad_client = "pub-xxxxx09818xxxxx";

google_ad_width = 728;

google_ad_height = 90;

google_ad_format = "728x90_as";

google_ad_channel ="117893460x";

google_ad_type = "text_image";

google_color_border = "336666";

google_color_bg = "669966";

google_color_link = "CCFF99";

google_color_url = "003333";

google_color_text = "FFFFFF";
```

```
//—></script>

<script type="text/javascript"

  src="http://pagead2.googlesyndication.com/pagead/show_ads.js">

</script></center></div>

<!— Begin #main — Contains main-column blog content —>
```

Before uploading, check the preview to make sure that the ads are where and how you want them, then "Save Template Changes" and "Republish" to refresh the blog.

Of course, you don't have to place AdSense directly above the text. **Another option is to embed the ads *within* the text so that they appear after particular entries**. That would limit you to three entries per page (if you wanted an ad unit after each entry) but it could increase your click-throughs.

## 9.4 Old Content

Blogs have to be written all the time, but if you've ever written anything in the past, don't just let it gather dust on your shelf. Give your old work a new lease of life by throwing it onto the Web!

For example, "Low Fat Linux" by Bob Rankin was written years ago. You may be able to find it on *Amazon.com*, but it's not likely that many people are buying it because you can read the entire book for free at *www.LowFatLinux.com*.

Bob's content has done its job of selling copies. Now it's doing a second job, selling clicks to ads.

What have you got lying around that could be earning you money?

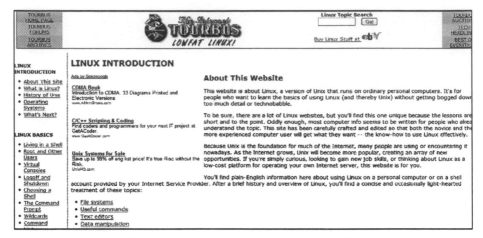

Fig. 9.1 Bob Rankin makes money from old notes. Note the position of his ads. They're prominent but could he get more clicks by putting them on the right? He could also have added an AdLink unit above the list of links on the left.

You might have an ebook of your own that isn't selling very well. Instead of attempting to sell your ebook for $19.95, why not turn it into web pages and make it available for free for all to enjoy?

Paste your AdSense code on the pages and you may make more from the ads than from sales of your ebook. Repurposing old content is a fantastic way to draw water from your own well.

I did this with a book that I'd written about online dating. The home page contains a list of chapter headings with a skyscraper ad on the left and a Google search box beneath it. There's also a banner on the top, which I expect people largely to ignore.

That ad does however make the ad unit look less commercial and the text ads match the list of chapter headings (although I used red for the links to match the color scheme of the page).

*Fig. 9.2 BestDates.info — Making money by using old content to bring people together.*

Note that this is a professional-looking website. That's important. The fact that you're using old content is no excuse for using an old design. You still have to make the page look good and pick up high-quality traffic if you want to get the clicks and the revenues.

On the internal pages, I've pushed the ads a little harder. Above the fold, there's no real content except for ads.

To stop people from scrolling away immediately though, I've used a nice big picture. I know that users will stop to look at that image. They'll then look at the ads and only after they've done that will they scroll down to read the page.

I've also put a long list of links on the left under the skyscraper to help the ads blend in and placed a third unit at the bottom of the page next to the free download.

*Fig. 9.3 Ads and an image above the fold at BestDates.info*

And the best thing about this strategy is that I've got so many pages of content to use. Each page is a separate chance to capture more clicks. I could even spin off the content on those pages and market them as individual articles or websites.

## 9.5 Volunteer Writers

To use old content, you have to have content in the first place. If you don't happen to have any out-of-print books that you've written lying around — and you don't feel like writing something new — another option is to ask people to write for your site for free.

Lots of people like writing. Just look at Amazon. They didn't pay a penny for all those book reviews. Their users write them for free and Amazon benefits.

When I started *www.WorldVillage.com*, I didn't have money to pay the people who reviewed software for me. Instead, I contacted the game companies and received complimentary copies of their computer games, which I then forwarded to a staff of volunteer writers. The agreement was that they would provide me with a written review of the game and they would keep the game as payment. I've got dozens of game reviews that bring users to my site and get them clicking on my ads. I didn't pay a penny for them but years later they continue to generate revenue for me.

You don't have to use reviews though. Whatever the subject of your website, you can add a line asking people to send in their thoughts and comments. You can just say something like: "We want YOU! We want your thoughts, articles and comments. Send your submissions to editor@yoursite.com and we'll post them here."

You can then create a whole new set of pages for your users' submissions and put AdSense on each one of them.

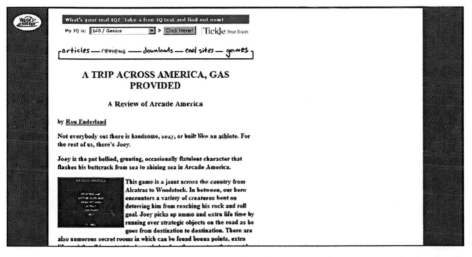

*Fig. 9.4 Game reviews at http://www.WorldVillage.com/softwarereviews/index.html*
*Mmm... free content.*

## 9.6 Build Thousands of Pages with Other People's Content

What is the focus of your web site? Is it all about parenting? Do you help people with their finances? Does your newsletter introduce people to new web sites? Or is your focus on the legal field? Regardless of your niche, you can benefit from taking advantage of one of the little-known secrets of AdSense experts... FREE syndicated articles.

Many writers want nothing more than to have their work published and read. Syndicated content is a dream-come-true for writers AND publishers. For the writer, it exposes their work to a larger audience. And for the publisher (that's you!), it means more quality content for your site. You might not be aware that there are literally THOUSANDS of articles available online which you can easily add to your web site!

Of course, the trick is knowing where to find these articles. Below is a list that can get you started by showing you where you can find over 30,000 articles that are ready to be placed on your own web site.

Please note that each site has its own restrictions and rules for using its content. In all cases, you must leave the author's name and web site link intact. Some sites require that you also link back to the site where you found the article. This is critical! Remember that while you are allowed to use the articles on your pages, the content is still property of the author. Please give credit where credit is due!

You may wish to publish articles only relevant to your topic, or you may wish to become a publishing powerhouse, adding thousands of new pages to your site. Regardless of how you wish to approach it, here are a few sites that provide you with thousands of FREE articles that you can republish on your web sites.

## EzineArticles.com

*www.eZineArticles.com*

A fantastic resources featuring over 100,000 articles covering a huge range of topics. However, they do have a limit of 25 articles/year for each site. Look through the categories and you can select some gems.

## DotComWomen.com

*www.DotComWomen.com/free-content.shtml*

Nice selection of articles targeting women.

## John Watson

*Members.Tripod.com/buckcreek*

John offers his stories for site owners to enjoy and place on their sites.

## ValuableContent.com

*www.ValuableContent.com*

The site name delivers as promises. Dozens of categories with hundreds of articles for you to publish. Marketing, business, humor, internet, legal, computing, sports, travel and many more.

## Patricia Fripp

*www.Fripp.com/articleslist.html*

Patricia Fripp is a businesswoman, marketer and motivational speaker. Her site offers over one hundred articles perfect for any business-oriented site.

## ArticleCity.com

*www.ArticleCity.com*

This one is a source of articles that will keep you busy for weeks on end. ArticleCity offers over 12,000 articles that you can place on your site. If the topic exists, you can bet that this site will have an article on that topic. I recommend spending a great deal of time selecting articles for your site here.

Want to find more? Simply do a Google search for "free articles" and see what turns up. Fine tune your search for your topic to find articles relevant to your site, such as "free parenting articles" or "free financial articles".

Now that you know where to find free content, you can build hundreds or thousands of keyword relevant pages and place your AdSense code on them to generate more revenue.

## 9.7  Add Public Domain Works To Your Site

One of the best kept secrets of free content comes in the form of Public Domain works.  Basically, these are books, articles, recordings and pictures whose copyrights have expired. Since they have not been re-registered with a copyright, they enter the public domain. What does that mean?  It means ANYONE (including you) can publish, re-publish and/or sell the works without paying a commission to anyone!

Think about this. You can build a site with HUNDREDS of pages just by publishing one public domain book on your site! Think of all the AdSense impressions you can deliver. The possibilities are endless.

I have two sources that you will want to investigate to find Public Domain works that you can begin using immediately

### Idea #1 — www.Gutenberg.org

Project Gutenberg is the oldest producer of free electronic books on the Internet. Their collection of more than 15,000 e-books was produced by hundreds of volunteers. As of this writing, the top 10 most popular works on Project Gutenberg are:

1. **The Notebooks of Leonardo Da Vinci by Leonardo da Vinci** at *www.Gutenberg.org/etext/5000*

2. **Project Gutenberg "10K" DVD** at *www.Gutenberg.org/etext/5000*

3. **How to Live on 24 Hours a Day by Arnold Bennett** at *www.Gutenberg.org/etext/2274*

4. **The Art of War** at *www.Gutenberg.org/etext/132*

5. **Ulysses by James Joyce** at *www.Gutenberg.org/etext/4300*

6. **The Adventures of Sherlock Holmes by Sir Arthur Conan Doyle** at *www.Gutenberg.org/etext/9551*

7. **Project Gutenberg "Best Of" CD August 2003** at *www.Gutenberg.org/etext/11220*

8.  **How to Speak and Write Correctly by Joseph Devlin** at *www.Gutenberg.org/etext/6409*

9.  **Alice's Adventures in Wonderland by Lewis Carroll** at *www.Gutenberg.org/etext/11*

10. **Grimm's Fairy Tales by Jacob Grimm and Wilhelm Grimm** at *www.Gutenberg.org/etext/2591*

Check out their entire library at *www.Gutenberg.org*.

**Please note that while you may republish these works on your site, you are not allowed to resell the works themselves.**

The downside of using works from Project Gutenberg is that hundreds of other people may already be using them. You might opt for less popular works in order to get better search engine placement.

# Idea #2 — The Lost Files at www.AdSense-Secrets.com/thelostfiles.html

Created by Russell Brunson, The Lost Files is a subscription-based service that provides the latest works to enter the Public Domain. In other words, he keeps you posted of new books and articles before everyone else gets their hands on them!

Here is a list of some titles available to members:

- How To Develop Self Confidence
- How To Draw and Paint
- Guide To Bowling
- What Character Does Your Handwriting Reveal
- How To Develop Perseverance
- How To Become A Speaker
- Dreams Interpreted
- How To Play Tennis

- Hints On Writing Short Stories
- How To Make Money
- Strength From Eating
- How To Study The Bible For Greater Profit
- The History Of Music
- How To Make and Use A Home Radio
- How To Write A Hit Song And Sell It

I have subscribed to this service and plan on testing some new public domain works on one of my sites. You can read more about The Lost Files at *www.AdSense-Secrets.com/thelostfiles.html*.

## 9.8 AdSense In RSS Feeds

One of the biggest changes to take place on the Internet recently has been the growth of RSS (Really Simple Syndication) feeds. These let subscribers see when a site has been updated and sends them information instead of waiting for them to come to the site to see it for themselves.

The good news is that Google is starting to put AdSense ads in RSS feeds.

The system is new and Google is still testing it as I'm writing this book but if you've got an RSS feed on your site (or want to set one up) and you've got more than a hundred subscribers, your site can join their team of Beta testers.

There seems to be little room for tweaking the ads, although it's a safe bet that the same principle of blending the ads into the page would apply as much here as on a Web page. At the moment though, the ads only appear after the content, at the bottom of the URL. You can apply for the program at *Services.Google.com/ads_inquiry/aff*.

Alternatively, if you don't want to be a Google guinea pig, Kanoodle is ahead of them. You can use their program at *www.Kanoodle.com/about/brightads.cool*.

## 9.9 Use Your Newsletter To Drive Traffic!

A great newsletter is another way to capitalize on AdSense. Newsletters are fantastic tools **to drive repeat visitors to your pages!**

Here's one way to use them: Instead of mailing the entire newsletter, save a few juicy tid-bits for your website and provide a link for your visitors to click.

When subscribers click-through to get the full story, they're likely to click your ads. And send you another AdSense bonanza! For example, Prizepot (*www.PrizePot.com*) is a contest and sweepstakes site with a new item each day. Their free weekly newsletter is sent with a teaser for all the new items posted that week. In order to find the entry form, you must click the link in the newsletter. Of course, when you arrive at the destination page, not only do you receive information about the contest, but you are greeted by AdSense ads. For a sample newsletter, send an email to *PrizePot@Aweber.com.*

> *If you have a big, responsive mailing list — start turning it now into extra AdSense cash!*

And if that isn't a good enough reason to start producing a newsletter, it looks as though Google is also testing AdSense in the newsletters themselves. They've already been doing it for *iVillage.com* and there's a good chance they'll be extending it to other users soon.

You can either create a newsletter yourself — and mail it using a mass mailing system like Intellicontact.com — or you can ask someone to write it for you. *ConstantConversions.com* is a copywriting service that specializes in newsletter writing. You can tell them about your site and they'll do it all for you, from concept to inbox. You can even tell them you want it optimized for AdSense. They'll know what to do.

To start your own email newsletter and auto-responder for your site, I highly recommend *Aweber.com*. With Aweber, you can build unlimited lists with unlimited autoresponders. That means you can have your list set up to automatically send email to certain groups at predetermined times. Along with their email broadcast services, Aweber is my first choice for many of my lists.

## 9.10  Buying Content / Hiring Writers

One of the problems with free content is that you can get what you pay for. And if your site doesn't have valuable content, it's going to have an effect on your click-throughs.

The alternative of course is to pay professional writers to write for you. I've already mentioned *www.elance.com* as a good place to find designers but it's a good place to find writers too. You can also ask *ConstantConversions.com* to write articles for you.

The advantage of hiring writers of course, is that you can be sure you're getting good content with little effort. On the other hand, you have to make that money back.

Try testing a writer to see how much profit a series of articles generates. If you pay $200 for five articles but find that your new pages don't give you a $200 increase in revenues, you either need a new idea — or a new writer.

## 9.11  Automated Content

Finally, another option you can use to build a website is automated content. This will let you cut through the hassle of creating a website from scratch, dreaming up content and driving traffic. For a fee, you'll be able to launch without delay a website filled with information and already optimized for search engines.

As long as your ads are bringing in more money than you're spending for the program, you're making a profit.

There are a number of programs you can use to do this. **ArticleBot** at *www.ArticleBot.com* automatically rewrites existing articles to create brand new versions that you can post on your site. While you can't take copyrighted articles as your originals, you can certainly use the tool to rewrite your own material and earn more cash by broadening your marketing, or by revamping public domain content.

While ArticleBot provides content, **MetaWebs** (*www.MetaWebs.com*) gives you the whole caboodle. You get a pre-built website already packed with content and SEO-optimized. In my opinion though, it's a good idea to swap the content that you get with the site for your own. It will bring you more dedicated users — and that's more likely to give you a higher income.

It's not a bad idea though to use a MetaWeb site to bring in money while you're creating your own material.

While MetaWeb and ArticleBot can certainly be used to generate AdSense revenue, **CashPageBuilder** (*CashPageBuilder.com*) was built specifically for AdSense. This is a very simple program to use. You can simply toss in a keyword phrase, choose the keywords and before you can say "How much is that worth?" you've got a site ready to roll.

And even if you choose a high-earning keyword that other people have chosen, you'll still get original content.

But there's a difference between original content and top-quality content.

The folks at Google aren't crazy about pre-fabricated, useless content and it's unlikely your users will be either. If all you're doing is building a site to earn money — and not because you're genuinely interested in the subject of your site — then maybe it doesn't matter. You can still launch your pre-fabricated site, post your ads in good places and send traffic to your advertisers.

It's worth remembering though that smart pricing (as discussed in chapter 11) was introduced precisely because of sites like these: sites with low-quality content get low advertising price. It's quite possible that having built your site, you'll find that the prices you receive will drop because you're not sending the advertisers users who are genuinely interested in their products.

The best way to ensure a high result from Smart Pricing is to give advertisers traffic that wants their product. Good content is the best way to do that.

If you are going to use pre-fabricated content though, then you can still try to keep the cost of your advertising space high by attracting good quality traffic. The users might not stay on your site for very long — and you don't really want them to — but if you can lay out your ads in such a way that when those users click off the site, they end up at an advertiser who does have the content they want to buy, you should still make money.

One thing you do have to be concerned about though is combining sites with pre-fabricated content in the same AdSense account as sites with high-quality content. If your Smart Pricing value does fall, then your income could fall across the board.

The best strategy if you're going to use these programs, I think, is to try to keep the sites you create with them in a separate account, when possible, and just make sure that your income is always higher than any monthly fee.

On the whole though, you'll probably find that it's more enjoyable and more lucrative to create websites that you enjoy maintaining and that users like visiting. Those are the sort of sites that make the most money.

# CHAPTER 10

# Response Tracking:
# Your Hidden Pot Of
# AdSense Gold!

# RESPONSE TRACKING: YOUR HIDDEN POT OF ADSENSE GOLD!

In the last chapter, we talked about content. Google won't let you ask visitors to click on your ads, or use other deceptive ways to make them click. But good content is an endorsement in itself. Some of its charm rubs off on the ads, making the ads more believable — and interesting!

If you have a website with impartial product reviews, for instance, visitors are more likely to click the ads to learn more about a product, check out the latest prices or order online.

It's crucial to create content that's genuinely interesting. But your work doesn't stop there.

After setting up your AdSense Account, the first thing you want to do is play with your ad formats and placement to make the ads blend in. That's where the bulk of the "easy-money" is hiding.

But once you've got that right, what next? You start tweaking the text and making all sorts of other changes to improve your CTR.

**But every time you make any sort of change to your ads, you must track the results.**

Consider this example:

Joe Drinker has a great website about "How to make Beer at Home". It's doing well on AdSense, but not well enough. His week's stats look something like this:

| Date | Page Impressions | Clicks | Page CTR | Page eCPM | Your earnings |
|------|------------------|--------|----------|-----------|---------------|
| 4/2/05 | 40930 | 1516 | 3.7% | 5.62 | 229.92 |
| 4/3/05 | 40358 | 1574 | 3.9% | 6.59 | 265.99 |
| 4/4/05 | 38962 | 1517 | 3.9% | 6.11 | 238.01 |
| 4/5/05 | 33563 | 1381 | 4.1% | 6.38 | 214.21 |
| 4/6/05 | 32978 | 1325 | 4.0% | 6.76 | 223.81 |
| 4/7/05 | 28207 | 1294 | 4.6% | 7.52 | 212.01 |
| 4/8/05 | 27322 | 1251 | 4.6% | 7.47 | 204.20 |

Joe is pretty happy with his CTR but wonders if he can raise his CPM and in the process, lift his earnings. So he looks up high-priced keywords related to his subject, and works the term "beer cans" into his content.

A few days later he logs into the stats on his AdSense account and finds that the change has actually HURT his income:

| Date | Page Impressions | Clicks | Page CTR | Page eCPM | Your earnings |
|------|------------------|--------|----------|-----------|---------------|
| 4/9/05 | 32744 | 985 | 3.0% | 4.21 | 137.95 |
| 4/10/05 | 32286 | 1023 | 3.2% | 4.94 | 159.59 |
| 4/11/05 | 30954 | 986 | 3.2% | 4.59 | 142.08 |
| 4/12/05 | 26850 | 898 | 3.3% | 4.78 | 128.52 |
| 4/13/05 | 26382 | 861 | 3.3% | 5.08 | 134.28 |
| 4/14/05 | 22566 | 841 | 3.7% | 5.63 | 127.20 |
| 4/15/05 | 21858 | 813 | 3.7% | 5.60 | 122.52 |

Joe has not only disappointed a lot of collectors who come looking for beer cans — his site contains lots of keywords but little in the way of good content — he has also discouraged visits from people who want to make beer at home.

His search ranking has gone down, making his website harder for people to find him and lowering his impressions. It's also hurt his earnings per click as the people who visit the site leave faster. What's worse is that he's also risked his AdSense standing!

Now, does that make it a bad idea to optimize your website for AdSense?

Not at all. It is actually a good idea, if you do it right. And by that I mean... No Shortcuts!

There is a simple, step-by-step process to optimize your website for high-paying search terms. And this method is almost fool-proof! So why isn't everybody doing this?

Simply because very few web publishers know how to use **Tracking** to their advantage. Tracking will not only help you minimize your mistakes, it will also reveal hidden pockets of money that you would have never found otherwise.

**Read on to find out how YOU can use Tracking to sky-rocket your CTRs and increase revenues per-click.**

*TIP:  Got to www.DigitalPoint.com/tools/adsense-sandbox/ to learn about FREE tools to optimize your website for high-paying search terms.*

## 10.1 How To Track With Channels

Google has its own FREE tracking feature called "Channels". Channels remind me of spy movies, where a smart chip is planted in the arm of a super sleuth, making it easier to track his activities or whereabouts.

AdSense now hands you 200 such chips. Use them to track ads on specific domain names or to group ads according to specific ad formats, keywords, their location on the page etc. You can use any other factor that might impact their effectiveness, based on the type of website you have.

*Channel those clicks!*

*Google tells you many things about each Channel, such as the ad impressions, click-throughs and earnings data.*

*You can use the channel reports to find out which channels are making you the most money — and how to increase your earnings for other channels.*

## 10.2 How To Create A Channel

**You should create a channel for each one of your sites.**

Within a site, you'll still have the option of creating channels for individual pages if desired, and this can be useful if you want to check how well ads are doing on a certain set of pages versus another set. But start by creating one URL channel for each site and you'll have the general overview that you can use as a starting point for your tracking.

And it's very easy to do.

The first thing you'll want to do is create URL channels.

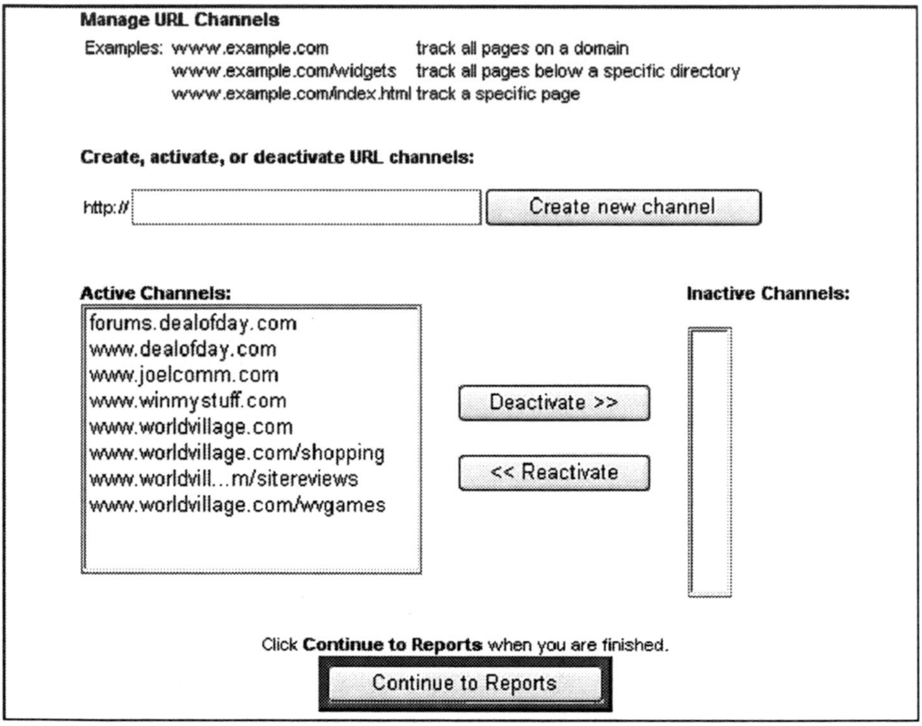

**Manage URL Channels**

Examples:  www.example.com          track all pages on a domain
www.example.com/widgets    track all pages below a specific directory
www.example.com/index.html track a specific page

**Create, activate, or deactivate URL channels:**

http:// [_____]    [ Create new channel ]

**Active Channels:**                                          **Inactive Channels:**

forums.dealofday.com
www.dealofday.com
www.joelcomm.com                    [ Deactivate >> ]
www.winmystuff.com
www.worldvillage.com
www.worldvillage.com/shopping       [ << Reactivate ]
www.worldvill...m/sitereviews
www.worldvillage.com/wvgames

Click **Continue to Reports** when you are finished.

[ Continue to Reports ]

*Fig. 10.1   Google gets powerful with URL Channels.*

The original Channels required you to **manually change AdSense tags** for each ad block you wanted to track. Many AdSense partners complained about the pesky old channels until Google launched its **URL Channels** to make life easier.

You can use URL Channels to track individual pages or just specify the domain name to track all the pages in that website.

The pages or websites you add will be automatically tracked — there's no need to manually change the code on those pages. Neat!

So if I need to track all the ad units appearing on my website *DealOfDay.com*, I just need to feed in the domain name and Google does the rest.

The URL Channels are especially useful if you have several websites, and have a general idea of the formats, colors, alignment etc. that works best for you.

Remember though, you still need the original, **Custom Channels** if you want to track ads across different domain names, based on ad sizes, formats, colors etc.

For instance, if I want to track left-aligned ads across all my websites (sites with different domain names), I need to group them together into a single channel and manually change the channel code for each page.

First, I name the new channel:

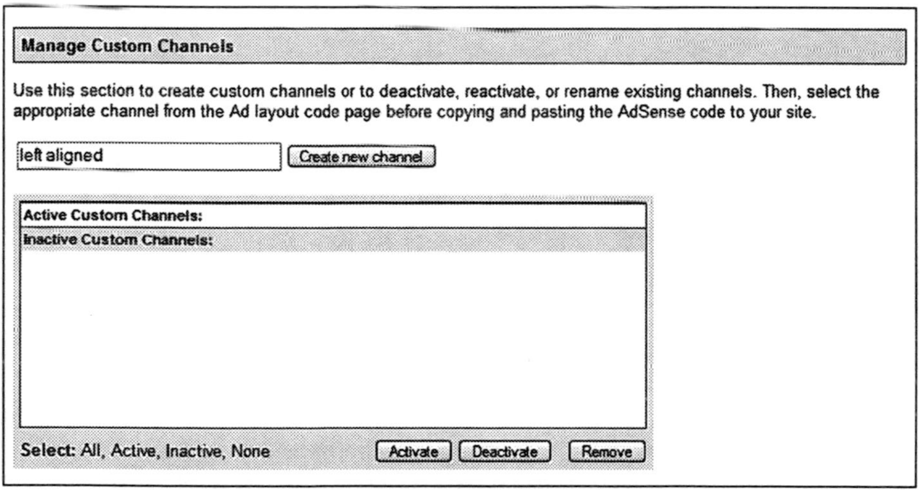

**Manage Custom Channels**

Use this section to create custom channels or to deactivate, reactivate, or rename existing channels. Then, select the appropriate channel from the Ad layout code page before copying and pasting the AdSense code to your site.

| left aligned | | Create new channel |

**Active Custom Channels:**
**Inactive Custom Channels:**

Select: All, Active, Inactive, None       [ Activate ]  [ Deactivate ]  [ Remove ]

*Fig. 10.2 Here comes a new channel...*

Then I choose the Ad Type, Layout and Color of the ads I want to track:

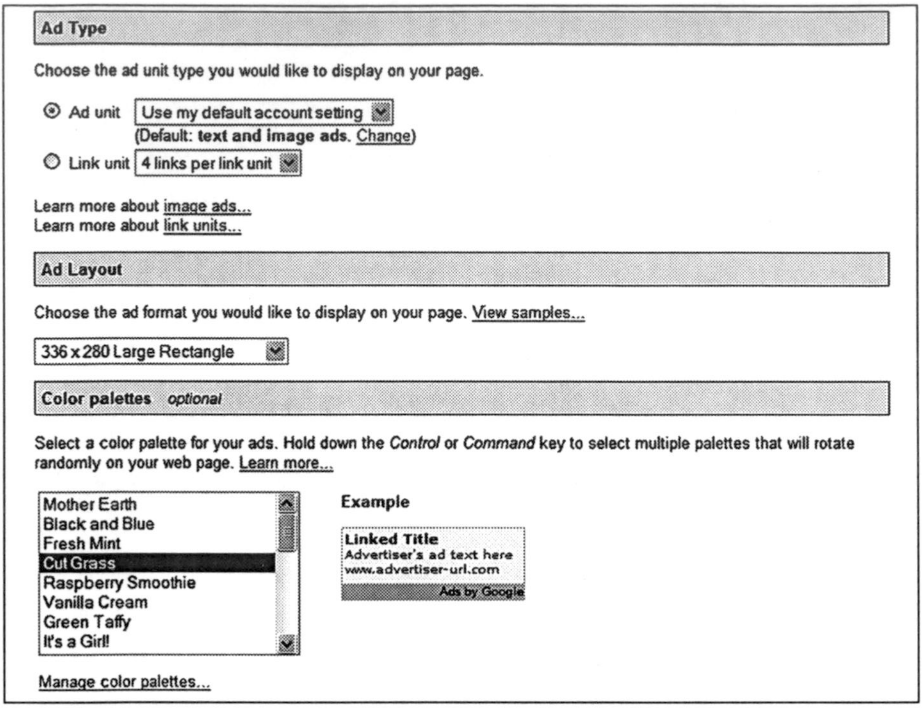

**Ad Type**

Choose the ad unit type you would like to display on your page.

- ⊙ Ad unit   [ Use my default account setting ▼ ]
  (Default: **text and image ads**. Change)
- ○ Link unit  [ 4 links per link unit ▼ ]

Learn more about image ads...
Learn more about link units...

**Ad Layout**

Choose the ad format you would like to display on your page. View samples...

[ 336 x 280 Large Rectangle ▼ ]

**Color palettes** *optional*

Select a color palette for your ads. Hold down the *Control* or *Command* key to select multiple palettes that will rotate randomly on your web page. Learn more...

| Mother Earth |
| Black and Blue |
| Fresh Mint |
| Cut Grass |
| Raspberry Smoothie |
| Vanilla Cream |
| Green Taffy |
| It's a Girl! |

**Example**

**Linked Title**
Advertiser's ad text here
www.advertiser-url.com
Ads by Google

Manage color palettes...

*Fig. 10.3 Defining the ads to track in my new channel.*

Finally, it's simply a matter of allocating an alternate URL if I don't want public service ads, selecting the channel and copying **and pasting the code onto each of the pages that contain these kinds of ad:**

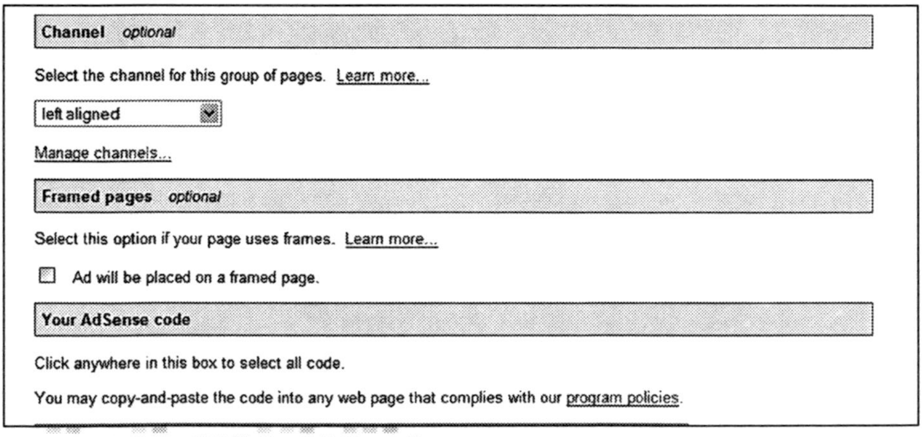

**Channel** *optional*

Select the channel for this group of pages. Learn more...

[ left aligned ▼ ]

Manage channels...

**Framed pages** *optional*

Select this option if your page uses frames. Learn more...

☐ Ad will be placed on a framed page.

**Your AdSense code**

Click anywhere in this box to select all code.

You may copy-and-paste the code into any web page that complies with our program policies.

```
<script type="text/javascript"><!--
google_ad_client = "pub-5618107640131804";
google_ad_width = 336;
google_ad_height = 280;
google_ad_format = "336x280_as";
google_ad_type = "text_image";
google_ad_channel ="3158925550";
//--></script>
<script type="text/javascript"
   src="http://pagead2.googlesyndication.com/pagead/show_ads.js">
</script>
```

*Fig. 10.4 Creating the code for my new Channel.*

Of course, I would then have to repeat the process if I wanted to track ads of a particular color or size.

While Google can now track ad performance for your specified domain name, please don't expect URL or Custom Channels to give you data about your visitors, such as who referred them to your website or which web browser they use. These are details only your server logs can tell you.

## 10.3  How To Read Your Server Logs

Various AdSense Tracking programs are currently sold on the Internet. This type of software runs on your own server which means it has access to vital visitor information.

These packages are not affiliated with Google, but you can use most of them without violating the AdSense TOS at *www.Google.com/adsense/localized-terms*.

External tracking software can tell you many things that the Channels don't reveal, such as:

■   Where your visitors are coming from

■   Where the ad-clickers are coming from

■   What search keywords led them to your web page

Your stats package should compile and interpret your log files. It will tell you how many people visited your pages, how long they stayed, which are the most popular pages, what countries/domains they visit from, and how many bookmarked your site.

Just about all the information you need.

One thing that external Tracking software **cannot** do for you, is to tell you **exactly how much MONEY** a specific ad (or a group of ads) is making for you. Only Google's Channels can tell you that.

External tracking software can tell you an ad's CTR, but your AdSense income also depends on factors such as the earnings per click, content relevance, your ranking on Google Search Results and many other factors besides.

> *I do recommend the use of external tracking software in addition to Google's Channels.*

Why? Because Channels can be quite confusing if you use them by themselves. Consider this example:

In this hypothetical case, Jim has a website about fast cars, where he discusses his passion with thousands of like-minded visitors. He decides to find out which ads are doing better than the others.

Jim groups all ads with a blue border into a specific channel, which he called "Blue_Border". He finds that the blue-border ads generated a 5% CTR (click-through ratio), while the rest of the ads generated around 2% CTR on average:

| Channel | Ad Unit Impressions | Clicks | Ad Unit CTR | Ad Unit eCPM | Your earnings |
|---------|---------------------|--------|-------------|--------------|---------------|
| Blue_border | 11378 | 569 | 5.0% | 7.24 | 82.38 |
| Green_text | 11205 | 525 | 2.0% | 6.29 | 70.54 |
| Tall ads | 12963 | 302 | 2.3% | 1.22 | 15.78 |

Next morning Jim tweaks all his ads to give them a blue border. The result?

The ads in the "Blue_Border" channel continue to generate 5% CTR, while the rest of the ads (which also have a blue border now) are still generating 2% CTR. Very confusing!

| Channel | Ad Unit Impressions | Clicks | Ad Unit CTR | Ad Unit eCPM | Your earnings |
|---|---|---|---|---|---|
| Blue_border | 11606 | 590 | 5.0% | 7.24 | 86.50 |
| Green_text | 11765 | 55 | 2.0% | 6.29 | 74.07 |
| Tall ads | 12315 | 287 | 2.3% | 1.22 | 14.99 |

Clearly, there's something else that's making Jim's visitors click — and it probably has nothing to do with the blue border.

**What is that hidden ingredient that's jacking up those click-through ratios? The Channels won't tell.**

Jim now decides to install an external tracking software on his website.

After looking through his server logs, he finds that ads with the term "Car Accessories" are getting the maximum click-throughs. How does Jim know that?

Simple. His tracking software tells him which ads his visitors are clicking. He also knows which sites his visitors are going to.

Jim found that of all his visitors, those who searched for the term "Car Accessories" were generating the maximum click-throughs on his web pages. Naturally, ads with the term "Car Accessories" were doing better than the others.

Should Jim now optimize his website for the search term "Car Accessories"?

For most web publishers, that's good enough to get down to work.

But Jim is skeptical. **Jim wants to know if his "Car Accessories" ads are also his top income generators**.

To find out, he creates a Channel to track the earnings of all ads with the term "Car Accessories" in it. He calls the new channel "Car_Accessories".

A few days later, Jim logs in to his AdSense account to check his earnings. He finds that about 30% of his income is drawn from visitors looking for car accessories.

| Channel | Ad Unit Impressions | Clicks | Ad Unit CTR | Ad Unit eCPM | Your earnings |
|---|---|---|---|---|---|
| Car Accessories | 14577 | 729 | 5.0% | 4.9 | 71.43 |

That's significant, but it raises another question in Jim's mind.

Where is the remaining 70% of his income coming from?

He looks through his tracking reports once again and finds that ads with the term "Car Parts" are also doing well. He found that while "Car Accessories" took the lead with 5% CTR, the "Car Parts" ads were generating a healthy 3% CTR.

Jim is excited. He knows he's on to something big!

Jim's tracking software has helped him uncover two great "leads". Which of these will lead him to his top income generator?

The plot thickens...

To find out, Jim now creates another channel called "Car_Parts".

A week later, he logs in to compare his earnings for each channel.

Here are Jim's results:

> Total AdSense income for one week = $1666.67
>
> "Car_Accessories" Channel = $500 (30% of total AdSense earnings)
>
> "Car_Parts" Channel = $1000 (60% of total AdSense earnings)
>
> Remaining Ads = $166.67 (10% of total AdSense earnings)

Incredible! Jim now knows that **his "Car_Accessories" ads might be getting him the most clicks, but his "Car_Parts" ads are making him the most money!**

Google won't tell you all reasons why the "Car_Parts" ads are making Jim more money. But Jim knows that the keyword "Car Parts" is probably more expensive, and that his website ranks better for that term.

FINALLY—

Jim is ready to act on this information. Let's take a look at his various options:

1.  He can use it to optimize his page for the search term "Car Parts", so that his content is more relevant. Jim knows from

experience that when his ranking for the search term "Car Parts" goes up, so will his earnings per click.

But it does have a downside. It might LOSE him his "Car Accessories" traffic! Jim knows that the price of keywords keeps fluctuating with the bids placed by AdSense advertisers. A keyword that's not so hot today can trigger a frenzied bidding war tomorrow!

Jim doesn't want to lose his most responsive visitors, earning him a decent $500 per week.

2.     Jim can optimize his page for "Car Accessories". But that comes with the huge risk of losing a whopping 60% of his earnings.

3.     Jim can launch dedicated web pages for "Car Parts" and "Car Accessories".

4.     Jim can optimize his page for BOTH search terms.

Jim decides to go with option 4 — optimize for BOTH search terms!

Jim knows the old saying that if you try to please everyone, you end up pleasing none at all. That's why he decides to play his cards carefully.

Jim understands visitor behavior. He knows that his visitors like to read in "bite sized" portions. They take a bite here and a nibble there. But they never read a web page like a book, starting from the top and reading right through to the bottom.

He tweaks his layout to make the "Car Parts" articles more visible. He smartly uses the hot car photos on his website to create several points of interest in his neatly laid out website.

Jim knows that people will instinctively look at the car photos, then be drawn in by detailed information about car parts — followed by the strategically placed Google ads.

To leverage this opportunity, Jim creates new space for content by tweaking the framework of his web page. Now Jim can capitalize his page layout by drawing people in with short, interesting 'content hooks' that build interest in the Google ads.

He adds new side-bars with juicy tid-bits about hot new car accessories. These will act like instant magnets to visitors looking for car accessories. More importantly, they run right alongside the AdSense ads, which tempt people with hot new offers on Car Accessories.

A specially designed "Accessories I love" section invites visitors to scroll down for more. Here Jim provides news, updates and impartial reviews about the Car Accessories Market. He entices visitors to check out new product launches with an integrated Google Search Box, which enables them to search within his website or search the entire web for relevant content.

These changes not only make Jim's web pages more relevant; it makes his visitors more receptive to the ads. And there's more. Jim can now create new income streams for himself by plugging in new links to pages dedicated to car accessories, car parts and other keywords that are already attracting highly responsive visitors to his existing pages.

Jim used his channels and server logs to drill deep and come up with a real gold-mine of information. You too can use these secrets to **zero in on ads that make you the most money** — and to find hidden sources of AdSense income.

## 10.4 Tracking Tools

There's a whole range of different tracking tools available to fill the gaps left by Google's Channels. Here is a quick run-down of the main ones:

### AdSense Log

*www.MetalGrass.com/adsenselog/index.html*

Created by MetalGrass, this stats analyzer has easy-to-read graphs and charts. They also use Google's own stats rather than tapping into your server's MySQL.

You can check your account as frequently as you want and the log will even you give you a sound, an email or a pop-up window when new data is available.

Price $50. Free 30-day trial.

## AsRep

*www.asRep.com*

AsRep lets you track all of your stats in real time. That includes each of your three regular ad units, an AdLink unit and up to two search boxes on each page.

The program also captures colors, format and channels, and whether the units are showing ads or alternates.

Price $50. Unlimited evaluation version available.

## CSV AdStats

*www.nix.fr/en/csvadstats.aspx*

CSV AdStats is less of a tracker and more of a number-cruncher. You can download Google's CSV data file and conduct a full stats analysis to check averages and create charts.

A useful way to squeeze more sense out of your stats.

FREE

## Google AdSense Tracking Script

*www.biz-directory.org/adsense/*

The Google AdSense Tracking Script lets you see the domains and files where clicks occurred, hourly and daily stats and who clicked what, where and when.

Price $100.

## *TWO TOOLS YOU CAN'T DO WITHOUT!*

If you are serious about making money with Google AdSense, there are two tools that you really need to download.

I was closely involved in the production of both of them.

I'd like to say that I didn't create these tools to make a profit, but that's not really true. I did create them to make a profit... but a profit as an AdSense publisher not as a software developer.

The fact is, none of the tracking software that I saw on the market was giving me all the information I wanted.

And I want to know everything!

I want to know where my users are coming from, what they're looking for, which ads they're clicking, how many unique visitors I'm receiving, which colors work best etc. etc.

With AdSense, I don't think it's possible to have too much information. No one was really willing to supply me the tools to gather and analyze that information. So I built them myself.

### AdSense Detective

The first of these tools is AdSense Detective.

I developed AdSense Detective, *AdsenseDetective.com*, together with my good friend, Robert Puddy, with *Focus4TheFuture.com*. We wanted that program to fill in all the knowledge and data gaps that we possibly could.

That's why in AdSense Detective, you'll be able to discover:

- Which domains, directories and pages of your websites users clicked
- The referring domains, pages and search terms that sent you visitors
- Which ad units, colors and formats were bringing you the most clicks

- The precise copy of the AdWords that you can check against page relevance
- The search terms used by visitors to find your page and...
- The exact AdSense channels of every ad clicked so that you can see which position on your page is bringing you the most money!

If you've got all that information, then frankly you've got everything you need to bring home the bacon.

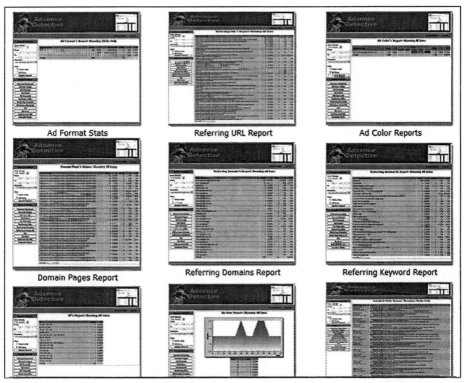

*Fig. 10.5 More data than you can shake a stick at from AdSense Detective.*

## AdSense Buddy

Of course, you still have to analyze and process all that data.

That's what my next tool does, and you can download it instantly.

As of this writing, AdSense Buddy is in beta and available for download at *www.AdSenseBuddy.com.*

The idea of the program is to make it as simple as possible for you to make sense of your stats. And because the program has been created by someone who not only knows AdSense, but uses it every day, you can be sure that it was made with the end user in mind so it should give you everything you could ask for.

If there's something I've left out, you probably don't need it.

You'll be able to follow your CTR and note your impressions. You'll be able to see your results by just rolling over the task bar. And I've even included an AdSense journal so that you can keep track of what's working and what isn't.

That alone makes it worth downloading.

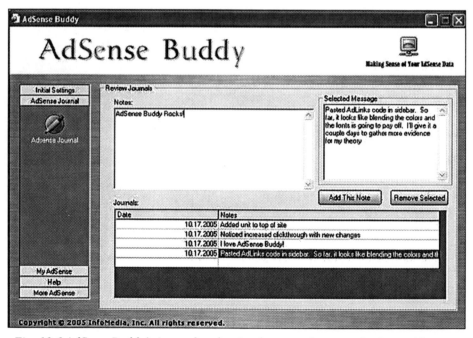

Fig. 10.6 AdSenseBuddy's journal makes it a breeze to keep track of your changes.

**132  THE ADSENSE CODE**

# *CHAPTER*
# *11*

# Smart Pricing... And What It Means For Your Income

# SMART PRICING... AND WHAT IT MEANS FOR YOUR INCOME

One of the more difficult aspects of using AdSense is keeping up to date with changes that Google likes to introduce from time to time. Most of these changes are pretty minor. That doesn't mean that you can ignore them — you will need to be aware of them. But you won't usually have to make massive changes to your site and the way you've optimized your ads when Google adjusts its policy.

One change that did have a dramatic effect on publishers took place in April, 2004: Google introduced Smart Pricing. We've already felt some of its effects in this book. Now we're going to explain exactly what it means...

First, let me just say that Smart Pricing was a pretty smart move, especially for advertisers. The principle is simple: before Smart Pricing, advertisers paid the price they had bid for each click their ad received on a website... regardless of whether that click resulted in a sale. The result was that some advertisers were receiving large numbers of clicks — for which they were paying large sums of money — but were seeing only a low return on that investment (ROI).

Not surprisingly, they were drifting away to other ad distributors, particularly Yahoo!, in the search for visitors who wouldn't just click but buy too.

To improve advertisers' ROI (and win them back from Yahoo!), Google lowered the price of ads on sites that tend to give advertisers few sales, even if they give them large numbers of clicks.

To put it another way, the same ad can now cost different amounts when it appears on different sites. And of course, **that same ad will pay publishers different amounts too**.

Before Smart Pricing, publishers had focused solely on attracting as many clicks as possible. With Smart Pricing, a site with a high CTR can still earn less than a site with a low CTR.

So how does Google measure an advertiser's conversion rate and what can publishers do to increase their conversion rates to ensure their ad rates remain high?

This is where things get tricky. Google is playing its cards pretty close to its chest when it comes to the methods it uses to calculate Smart Pricing and even measure ROI.

## 11.1  *What Google Has Said About Smart Pricing*

This is what Google has officially told us about Smart Pricing:

■ **The price of an ad is influenced by a number of different factors.**

Those factors can include: the bid price; the quality of the ad; competition from other ads in the same field; the location of the ad as part of a marketing campaign; "and other advertiser fluctuations."

■ **The ad price is <u>not</u> affected by the clickthrough rate.**

Sending advertisers large numbers of clicks will not increase the bid price. (That doesn't mean that CTR isn't important at all for your revenues; it's just not important in determining the amount you receive for the click.)

■ **"Content Is King."**

Google makes it pretty clear that sites that will benefit most from AdSense are those that "create compelling content for interested users." They also emphasize the importance of bringing targeted traffic to look at that content. Those are two different factors which together create a site with loyal, appreciative users. Just the sort of thing that every serious webmaster wants.

## 11.2 What Else Do We Know About Smart Pricing?

What Google has told us about Smart Pricing isn't much. It also raises at least as many questions as it answers: How does Google judge the quality of an ad? How can they tell the role an ad plays in a marketing campaign? What are the other "advertiser fluctuations"? And perhaps most importantly, how do they track the results of the clicks?

All of those pieces of information would be very useful to a publisher. But Google wasn't letting on.

Fortunately, publishers caught a break. Jenstar, the author of an excellent contextual advertising blog at *www.Jensense.com*, (you should definitely make this site a part of your regular reading) was contacted by an advertiser who was being tempted back from Yahoo! to Google. He told Jen what the AdSense salesman had told him about Smart Pricing. She told us.

This is what it boiled down to:

■ **Smart Pricing is calculated across an AdSense account.**

So if you have a number of different sites covering a range of different topics and one of them delivers a low ROI, all of your ad prices may be lowered.

■ **Smart Pricing is evaluated weekly.**

If you believe that an ad is delivering a low ROI, you can remove it from your site and you should see higher ad prices within a week.

■ **Smart pricing is tracked with a 30-day cookie.**

Users don't have to convert immediately into a sale (or whatever will count as a conversion) for you to benefit. They can think about it for a month and you'll still get the benefit.

- **Image ads are affected by smart pricing**.

  Few serious publishers use image ads except when they're receiving CPM campaigns. Was this a reference to ads in low locations receiving lower rates?

- **Prices may be reduced even below an advertiser's minimum bid**.

  So looking up the bid prices for targeted keywords won't help you very much; if your ROI is low, your rates could be lower than the minimum quoted.

- **Conversions accounts are tracked by advertisers opting into AdWords Conversion Tracking**.

  But we still don't know what Google is tracking or how it's making calculations with its results.

## 11.3 Strategies To Benefit From Smart Pricing

The challenge for publishers trying to keep their ad rates high is that there's no way to know exactly how many of your clicks are converting into sales for your advertisers. You can't even tell what would *count* as a sale for the different advertisers you're promoting.

The best you can do is keep track of your clicks and your revenues, and make sure that they rise and fall at the same rates.

If following your stats was always important, Smart Pricing has made it absolutely vital. There's little point in spending hours trying to increase your CTR if the value of your clicks is dropping like a rock.

So what should you do if you notice that your income is dropping but your CTR rate remains the same?

The first thing you should do is protect yourself. Because one site with a low ROI can affect all the sites in your account, dividing your sites between different accounts would prevent all of your revenues falling if one site underperforms. Officially, that's a breach of TOS, so you can't really do it

But I don't see why two different sites can't be owned by two spouses. If you own more than two sites though... well, I guess you're stuck.

Next, if you suspect that one page has a low ROI, try removing the AdSense code from that page, wait a week and see if you can spot an improvement in your ad prices. If there's no improvement, replace the code and try taking the code from a different page. You want to find the page that's poisoning your earnings and keep AdSense ads off it until you can bring in the kind of traffic that suits your advertisers.

And that's where you're most likely to find the underperforming pages. **The pages that are most likely to have the greatest conversion rates for advertisers are those that have the most loyal following.** The closer the connection between your site and the interests of your visitors the more likely they are to click on your ads — and buy when they click.

So it's also a good idea to create niche sites that appeal to niche audiences, rather than general sites that bring in audiences interested in a bunch of different things. Those sorts of users will also only have a vague interest in some of the things on your site and could lower your conversion rate.

You might have a blog, for example, in which you discussed your interests in... oh, dogs, computer games and the movies of Mel Gibson. That would bring in users with three different kinds of interests... and three different kinds of ads. But a dog-loving user who clicks on an ad for Mel Gibson DVDs is less likely to actually buy than a Mel Gibson fan. Your conversion rate would drop and the value of every ad you promote would fall too.

But if you created three separate blogs, one for each of your interests, you would receive fewer false clicks, and a higher rate of conversion.

Ultimately then, the ideal strategy is, as always, to create good content that attracts genuinely interested users.

*Don't remove the AdSense code from pages with low CTR; remove it from pages with low ROI!*

# CHAPTER 12

# How To Make
# AdSense Work With
# Internet Communities

# HOW TO MAKE ADSENSE WORK WITH INTERNET COMMUNITIES

## *Maximize your AdSense Revenue from Internet Forums, Message Boards and Discussion Groups!*

Earlier in this book, I mentioned making revenue from blogs. But blogs certainly aren't the only types of content online or the only types that can use AdSense.

In an active Internet Community, users generate most of the content.

You cannot completely control the keywords or the topics, which means AdSense might spring some surprises with the ads that show up. (Just have some Alternate Ads handy, in case AdSense pulls up a series of non-paying public service ads.)

Unlike passive surfers who like to explore your website for relevant information, forum members are very focused on their messages and the responses they attract.

Many publishers that play host to Internet Communities complain of negligible CTRs, scattered keywords (low content relevance) and low cost per click. What they don't realize is that Internet Communities are a hidden gold-mine which inspire fanatical loyalty, repeat visits, unique content and a high level of user involvement with the content.

Mega-brands such as Apple and Harley Davidson were built on the same foundation — a deep sense of personal bonding, high involvement with the product and strong referrals. You can achieve the same result with your website!

While all Internet Communities are not the same, they do have the same key strengths. You just need to recognize them and find new ways to cash in on them — as some savvy web publishers are doing already!

## 12.1 Google's Forum Heat Map

Just as Google produced a heat map for standard websites, they've done the exact same thing for forums. You can find that map, together with their suggestions at *http://adsense.blogspot.com/2005/10/six-adsense-optimization-tips-for.html.*

Google's tips are usually quite sensible. They recommend that a skyscraper on the left is a good idea and that horizontal ads beneath should be placed beneath each forum entry. They also suggest putting a leaderboard at the bottom of the page, but before the footer, and opting in to take image ads.

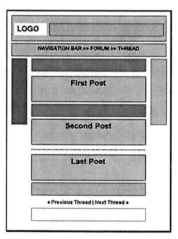

*Fig. 12.1 Google's Forum Heat Map.*

I'm not sure about all of those suggestions though. Here's why:

■ Forum Members are very focused on their topic of discussion. **Ads that appear on the top, bottom or side margins of the page may not distract them from their main objective —** which is to read and write the posts!

- The best way to capture their attention is to **put your ads at the end of the top posting on each page**. Posts that appear on top are read more often, and usually set the tone for the rest of the discussion.

  Many web publishers swear by **Google's 728x90 leaderboard ad with two ads trailing top-of-the-page posts**.

- What gets the most clicks in any forum?

  The **forum buttons** of course! Put your ads close to these useful buttons, sought out by users to search threads, create a new thread or post a reply. Check out this example:

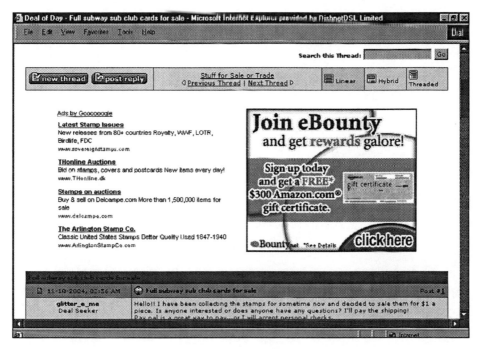

*Fig. 12.2  Positioned under the vital forum buttons, these Google Ads attract users in the right frame of mind- when they're ready to click! Turn to the next page for another great way to make your Google Ads more 'clickable'!*

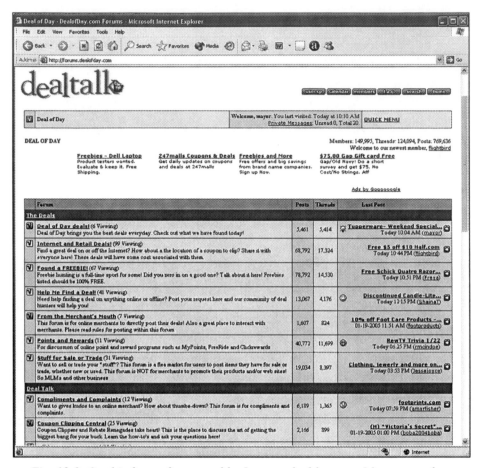

Fig. 12.3 On this forum frequented by Internet deal hunters, I have turned my
Google text ads into the hottest 'star attraction'. Forums.DealOfDay.com

Without ever asking users to click, **the heading "Deal of Day"
turns the Google Ads into a recommended resource for finding
the day's top deals**.

Impressive forum stats, such as the number of members, threads and
posts appear alongside the ads, making them look more legitimate. The
sheer number of users creates a sense of urgency to check them out
before other members get their hands on the coveted deals!

- Make sure you **apply the same text formatting as the user-generated content**. It's important to gain your users' attention first — then pitch your message when they're all ears!

- Try putting the ads **at the bottom of each post**. If users spot the pattern and your click-throughs start to drop, try putting the ads at the bottom of every alternate post. The key is to keep them guessing!

- **Don't break up a post by putting ads in the middle.** Since forums have user-generated content, people are more sensitive to these intrusions and might be offended if you make it seem as if the ads are their personal recommendations.

- **Don't lump a bunch of ads together in the middle of the page**. It works well with 'passive' visitors, but your forum members will read right around them!

- **Allow users to pull up targeted ads with a Google Search Box!** How often has a forum posting piqued your interest enough to launch a Google search? Once? Twice? All the time? If you're anything like me, **the Google Search Box is an added convenience, welcomed by most users**. It makes your visitors stay! And if they click an ad from the results page, you make money!

*Which of these strategies will work for your Forums?*

Only time can tell — but don't forget to track your results with Google's FREE AdSense Channels. There are publishers who have made a fortune with their community pages. It doesn't take rocket science. But a little persistence goes a long way!

# CHAPTER 13

# How To Read Your
# Visitors Like A Book

# HOW TO READ YOUR VISITORS LIKE A BOOK

## 13.1 Making Sense Of Stats, Logs And Reports...

Stats are a vital part of your success. If you can't follow the results of all the changes you're going to be making to your ads and your pages, then you're never going to maximize your revenues.

But reading your stats can be confusing. You're going to be staring at all sorts of tables filled with all kinds of numbers which can be rearranged and reorganized in all sorts of different ways. That's why it's crucial to know how to read your stats and understand the figures.

## 13.2 The Most Important Stat Of All

There's one figure that's more important than any of the others. Know which one I'm talking about?

Revenue! If you aren't making money, no other stats matter.

If you are making money though, the next stat you want to watch is your CTR. The higher the percentage of clicks to page impressions you receive, the higher your CPM will rise — and the higher your revenues will become.

When you make a change to your ad placement, to your keywords, to your ad colors or anything else, wait a week and check your stats to see the result. And look first at your revenues.

Bear in mind too that when you have multiple ads on a page each ad unit counts as one impression — but you won't be able to get three clicks from them! Multiple ad units then can reduce your CTR while still giving you good revenues.

You might also want to translate your results into charts. If you do want to do that, the most important things to look for are trends in CTR and in earnings. Tracking impressions too will also let you see any radical fluctuations in traffic.

## 13.3  Optimum CTR

Much of your success will depend on lifting your CTR as high as possible. Obviously, the more people who click on your ads the more money you should make but it's not always easy to know when you're inviting as many people as possible to get clicking. I've gone from less than 1% CTR to over 8% on some sites but I know of some sites that are getting over 30% CTR!

Your CTR will depend on a number of different factors, including:

- **Site Content** — some types of content get more clicks than others (but don't necessarily make more money per click...)

- **Site Design** — we've already talked about the importance of where you place your ads and how you place them

- **Number Of Links** — why give your ads competition? If people want to click away from the page, you should get paid for it

- **Ad Relevancy** — If you're not getting served ads that are relevant to your content, you're going to have a low CTR

## 13.4  AdSense Arbitrage

Once you get to grips with the numbers that you see on the stats pages and your logs, you might notice something interesting. You might see for example, that you're getting 5,000 ad clicks on a page each month and that page is generating $1500.

Divide $1500 into 5,000 clicks and you'll realize that each click for that type of content is bringing you 30 cents.

That means that when you come to buy content, as long as you spend less than 30 cents for a click to that page, you're going to make a profit. And one way to do that is to open an AdWords account and buy advertising space on Google's search pages. You could pay as little as 5 cents per click, giving you a profit of 25 cents each time your 5-cent users click on your 30-cent ads.

That's AdSense arbitrage and it sounds like a foolproof way to increase your revenues.

If it were that easy, everyone would be doing it.

The first problem with arbitrage is that you can never get a 100% CTR. Not every 5 cent click you buy is going to give you 30 cents back — and every impression that doesn't result in an ad click is going to eat into your profits.

With these kinds of figures (and obviously, yours are going to be different), you'd need a 16% CTR to break even. (If every ad click costs 5 cents and gives you 30 cents, you can afford to lose five out of every six clicks or 16%).

So if you can see that you're getting a 16% CTR, buying advertising on AdWords to send traffic to your AdSense ads could be a good deal.

Or not.

The second problem with arbitrage is that your CTR rate is based on users coming from your current traffic sources. The users you buy through AdWords might behave differently. They've already clicked on an ad once so they might not want to click on an ad again. Or alternatively, because you know they're the type who do click on ads, it's possible that they're exactly the type who'll click on the ads on your page.

Results from using arbitrage vary. Some people report that the clicks they buy on AdWords give them less revenue, others report that they've increased their CTR.

The real key to arbitrage success is buying traffic based on the right keywords. And to do that you need...

## 13.5 WordTracker

WordTracker is a great way to find keywords to target for arbitrage. The idea is simple: if you can find popular keywords that few sites are targeting, you can increase the CTR of the ads you buy *and* improve the chances that users will click on the ads on your page. It's those keywords that will give you the best revenues for arbitrage-and the most clicks from search engine listings.

WordTracker actually helps in four different ways.

First, you enter a keyword-say, "football". WordTracker will then give you a list of *hundreds* of different keywords related to football-words like "stadium" and "team" and "football player". Some of those words you'll probably have thought of, but lots of them you won't.

**Now you have already got more keyword options than when you started!**

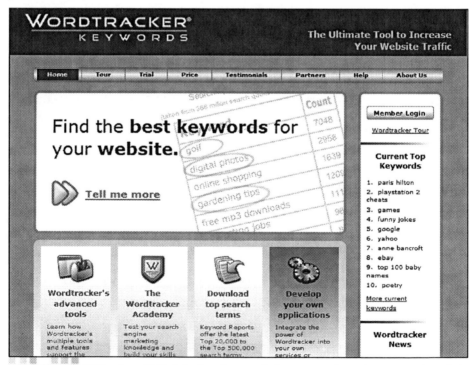

*Fig. 13.1 WordTracker: "Find the best keywords for your website". Says it all really!*

The next step is to see how popular these keywords are. WordTracker looks across all of the main search engines and tells you how many people searched for each keyword in the last 60 days. That's certainly interesting information in itself but there's not much point in targeting a word that 1,000 people search for every couple of months if a million Web pages are already targeting it.

Your ad would appear on page fifty-something of a search engine listing and get very few clicks.

The next stage is where things get really interesting. **WordTracker compares the number of searches that people are making for each keyword with the number of sites targeting that keyword**.

It even awards each keyword a score that indicates the size of the opportunity for new pages that want target that particular keyword. It then becomes easy for you to see which words are likely to give the best search engine listings-and which will get the most clicks for the lowest prices when you pay to advertise.

For example, if you asked WordTracker to look up the word "football," you might find that 3,474 people look for "shoulder pads" each day but only 2,375 Web pages are targeting that word. If one of the pages of your football site targets that keyword, you're almost certainly going to find yourself high on the search engine listings, giving you plenty of free traffic.

But if you also choose to pay to advertise your site on a GoogleAd, you can be confident that you'll get plenty of clicks-and great revenues.

WordTracker is a fantastic tool. It should definitely be in your money-making toolkit. Take a look at it at *www.WordTracker.com*.

# CHAPTER 14

# What To Do Before You Apply To Google AdSense

# WHAT TO DO BEFORE YOU APPLY TO GOOGLE ADSENSE

## *(Guidelines for new web publishers)*

Imagine this. Mr. Big Google Advertiser is surfing the net, looking up some trade-related keywords. He clicks through lazily to land on a strange website. The logo looks amateurish. The content is full of typos. Heck, some of the links don't even work. And then, he sees something he least expects to find.

He seems to freeze for a second. His eyes pop wide open and you can see a muscle going in his cheek. He picks up his phone and dials a number. "I can't believe it!" He booms, "I can't believe you put MY ad on THAT website!"

Uh oh.

Google has a reputation to live up to. A reputation for providing quality content, targeted traffic and good value for money to their advertisers.

The way to meet these requirements is to provide content that meets their requirements and goes one step further to add something unique, which other websites might not offer.

*Before you apply to Google AdSense, make sure you haven't cut corners on the layout and the quality of content. Google is quick to reject websites that are built specifically to attract search spiders or that trick people into clicking AdSense Ads.*

To make a sizable income from AdSense, you need unique content, a true commitment to your visitors and **focused content** — which makes it easy for advertisers to target their audience.

To sum up, here are a few quick Do's and Don'ts before you Apply:

## 14.1 Don't Build A Website That Specifically Targets Search Spiders, With Nothing Unique To Offer Human Visitors.

I've already discussed the importance of creating content that your users are genuinely going to find interesting. If you have interesting content, you'll have higher CTR and higher revenues.

With so many legitimate ways of creating revenue-generating content, you're only cheating yourself when you take a short-cut. You reduce your CTR and you increase the odds of being banned by Google.

## 14.2 Don't Build A Website Just To Make Money From AdSense

The easiest way to produce genuinely interesting content is to produce content that genuinely interests you!

You might feel that the more pages that you can throw up, the more money you'll make but if you can't produce the sort of content that can compete with companies who produce genuinely good material, you're not going to get the traffic or the revenues.

But there is plenty of topics that you know about and enjoy. That's the kind of material that can give you money. It will also make earning that money a lot more fun.

## 14.3 Provide Targeted Content That Will Help Google Advertisers To Capitalize Your Traffic

But writing about what you enjoy rather than what can help you earn doesn't mean you should forget about using your content to bring you targeted ads.

If you know that there are certain keywords in your topic that are worth more, then you can certainly write about those. You can also make sure that you toss in plenty of keywords and headings to keep those ads targeted.

## 14.4 DON'T Build A Website Specifically To Target High-Value Keywords <u>Unless</u> You Plan On Developing Quality Content!

**Not all advertisers bid high on the same keywords.**

Just as it's a bad idea to create more content simply to create more money, so it's a mistake to focus on particular keywords to create lots of money!

If you are prepared to produce good content and want that content to include high value keywords, one VERY useful report reveals those high-value keywords. You can find it at: *http://www.adsense-secrets.com/cashkeywords.html*

| # | Keywords | Avg Bid | Searches | Results | R/S Ratio | Google Ads | CPD |
|---|----------|---------|----------|---------|-----------|------------|-----|
| 1 | new orleans real estate | $19.74 | 11,147 | 2,310,000 | 207 | 45 | 7.0 |
| 2 | cleveland ohio real estate | $12.16 | 14,779 | 1,550,000 | 105 | 39 | 0.9 |
| 3 | nashville real estate | $9.07 | 18,040 | 3,090,000 | 171 | 50 + | 9.6 |
| 4 | real estate license | $8.73 | 23,826 | 6,390,000 | 270 | 42 | 61.2 |
| 5 | orlando real estate | $8.45 | 13,584 | 4,680,000 | 345 | 50 + | 14.0 |
| 6 | real estate lawyer | $7.75 | 13,414 | 9,740,000 | 726 | 38 | 6.2 |
| 7 | real estate school | $7.22 | 37,874 | 16,300,000 | 430 | 46 | 52.2 |

*Fig. 14.1 Sample report revealing high-value keywords.*

If you want to aggressively build sites, another very useful tool you might want to look at is **Top Keyword Lists**.

This is a 'plug and play' monthly membership service offering twenty-five high-paying AdSense markets each and every week. With a simple page generating application, you can turn out twenty-five sites quickly and easily from each week's updates. If you prefer to spend a little more time building your site with articles, they offer a unique keyword research tool that allows you to pinpoint the key phrases you should concentrate your articles on for maximum payout through AdSense. Read more about it at *www.adsense-secrets.com/topkeywords.html*

## 14.5 Websites That Rank Higher In A Google Search (SERPS) Will Get A Better Per-Click Payout Than Websites Which Rank Lower For The Same Search Term

I don't know if that's because Google just wants to reward sites who meet their criteria for high search listings or because they assume that sites that rank higher are going to have better users for advertisers than lower-ranked sites.

**Most likely though, is that it's all about content relevance**. A top-ranking website is considered more relevant than a lower-ranking one. So keep an eye on your Google Search Ranking for your targeted search terms and work continuously to optimize your website. The upshot is that when you've created your site, you need to pay attention to search engine optimization.

That won't only win you free traffic, it will also get you more money for the traffic you receive.

You can learn more about search engine optimization in chapter 17.

## 14.6 Increase 'Readiness to Buy'

Advertisers prefer websites that qualify visitors for the purchase.

Allow me to explain with this simple example: A search for "cell phones" can throw up a page about the perils of cell phone radiation, a university professor's treatise about messaging technologies and a buyer's guide that compares features and prices of top-selling cell phone models.

For an advertiser looking to target cell phone buyers, the buyer's guide offers the most relevant (and therefore **valuable**) advertising space.

This is part of targeting your content.

You want people to click on your ads. So do your advertisers.

If you can keep your content focused on the products your advertisers are selling then you should be able to increase your CTR.

Of course, it's also Google's job to make sure that your ads match your content, but if you're writing about DVD's it makes sense to produce content that encourages people to buy DVD's because those are the sort of ads you know you're going to be served!

If you were writing about home buying, you can be sure that you'd get ads about mortgages and real estate agents. Put up pages about finding the right mortgage or how to pick a real estate agent and not only do the ads look even more relevant, they'll also appear more attractive.

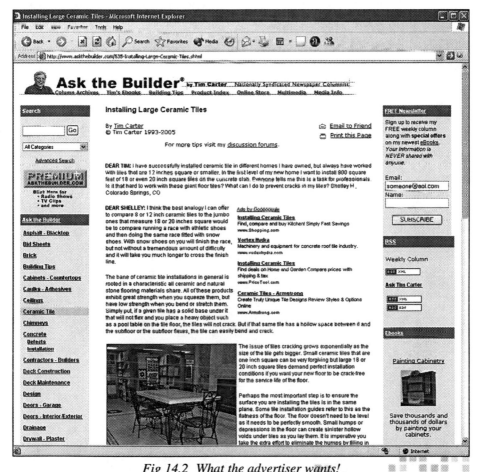

*Fig 14.2 What the advertiser wants!*

Tim Carter is a living example of how content relevance builds loyalty. As an expert in his field, he adds relevance and credibility to the ads appearing on his pages. Check out this example at: *http://www.AskTheBuilder.com/535-Installing-Large-Ceramic-Tiles.shtml.*

## 14.7 Don't Cut Corners!

Watch out for typos, amateurish layouts, malfunctioning links, poor-quality or plagiarized content.

Users expect to reach professional websites. Those are the ones they spend the most time on and pay the most attention to. Those are also the ones that Google rewards the most.

It pays to put effort into improving your website. It pays to have a good design and a site that's attractive and well-maintained.

# CHAPTER 15

# Recommended Resources:
# Try These Tools And
# AdSense Utilities (Some Are FREE!)

# RECOMMENDED RESOURCES: TRY THESE TOOLS AND ADSENSE UTILITIES (SOME ARE FREE!)

## (Making life easier for AdSense Partners)

### 15.1 Test Your Mettle With The AdSense Sandbox!

Before you apply to AdSense, put your web pages through a 'mock-test' with a FREE web utility called the AdSense Sandbox at *www.digitalpoint.com/tools/adsense-sandbox*. It's a great way to determine what type of ads your pages pull up. You can also estimate your earnings potential from the keywords in the ads.

The AdSense Sandbox is free to use, requires no subscription and displays results with a single click.

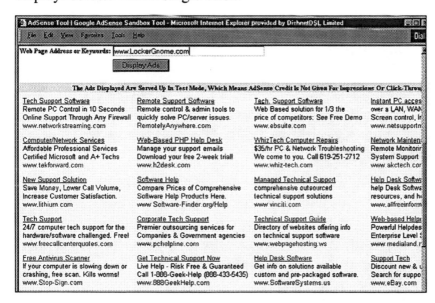

*Fig 15.1*

*Fig 15.1 I tested the AdSense Sandbox with Chris Pirillo's website www.LockerGnome.com and was presented with a list of 20 ads. The actual website has 4 ads, **all of which were displayed by the Sandbox**.*

Many AdSense partners are already using it — with excellent results! Go here to try it, Free! *www.DigitalPoint.com/tools/adsense-sandbox/*

## 15.2 Google AdSense Preview Tool

*www.Google.com/support/adsense/bin/answer.py? answer=10004&topic=160*

If you have Windows Internet Explorer (version 6 or higher), you can now install this neat tool provided by Google to check out ads that are most likely to show up on your web page.

It takes just a few clicks and works with any web page — even if you still haven't got AdSense.

## 15.3 Overture Bid Tool

*uv.bidtool.overture.com/d/search/tools/bidtool/ index.jhtml*

While Google won't disclose what each click is worth, you can try indirect methods such as the Overture Bid Tool to find out the relative cost of different keywords at *http://uv.bidtool.overture.com/d/search/ tools/bidtool/index.jhtml*.

Overture Bid Tool displays the relative amounts that each Overture (*http://www.Overture.com*) advertiser is willing to pay 'per click' for a specific keyword. You can compare maximum bids for different keywords to arrive at an educated guess about the most profitable keywords for your website.

Remember that what Google actually pays you may vary greatly. But you will get closer with practice! ;)

## 15.4  Overture Keyword Suggestion Tool

*inventory.overture.com/d/searchinventory/suggestion/*

Enter a search term and Overture tells you how many times it was looked up on Overture during the previous month. It will also give you a related list of keywords including how many searches were carried out for each search term in the list.

## 15.5  Ultimate SEO Tool

*www.Googlerankings.com/ultimate_seo_tool.php*

Just feed it your website address and hit Enter. This amazing tool will show you a list of the most frequently used words and phrases, including detailed reporting of the number of times it appeared as well as the keyword density. Then, hit the "Create Position Report" button to check how your website ranks for each search term. (Can you ask for more?)

## 15.6  Google AdWords Traffic Estimator and Bid Tool

*adwords.Google.com/select/TrafficEstimatorSandbox*

If you are an AdWords Advertiser, you can use this tool to get the estimated bid price and traffic for your desired list of search terms.

## 15.7  Keyword Rankings Tool

*www.Googlerankings.com/index.php*

How does your site rank on Google search for a specific search term? Find out with this free tool.

## 15.8  Mass Keywords Search

*www.Googlerankings.com/mkindex.php*

Find out how your website ranks on Google for up to ten different keywords — in one go! If you'd also like to study the top 100 sites for your specific search keyword, you'll get the results even faster!

## 15.9  Guide to Google-friendly Design

*www.Googlerankings.com/Googlefriendly.php*

You see a beautiful website with great content. But Googlebot spots heaps of nonsense code hidden behind the scenes. Your Google ranking depends on a combination of words, design and programming. Find out how to create a relevant, clean and clutter-free website: the kind that Googlebot loves!

# CHAPTER 16

# Keeping Track Of What Works — And What Doesn't Work — For You!

# KEEPING TRACK OF WHAT WORKS — AND WHAT DOESN'T WORK — FOR YOU!

## (Start An AdSense Journal)

People who want to lose weight often keep a "food diary". Without a food diary, it's easy to forget that late-night snack or the extra sugar in your fourth cup of coffee. A food diary keeps you honest. It helps you figure out the real reasons behind those little ups and downs in your weight.

I'm sure that after reading this book, you would be eager to try out many of the tweaks discussed in here — including some of your own.

*Without an AdSense journal, it would be easy to undo your successes, or to repeat your failures. Remember the program that I mentioned earlier, AdSenseBuddy. This tool provides everything you need to keep an ongoing journal of your AdSense activity!*

Every little tweak counts, but don't try to do everything at once.

Take the step-by-step approach. Write your own AdSense plan for the first week. Log into your AdSense account once a day, to track your click-throughs and earnings.

Don't be rigid about your plan. Make room for inspiration. If you've got a great idea, write it down to implement it later. Don't implement your ideas all at once and DO give every idea some time to prove its mettle. You'll find out within a day if you have thousands of visitors hitting your web pages. If that is not the case, give it a few days. Preferably one week!

Don't be discouraged by minor, day-to-day fluctuations in your click-throughs and earnings. It's normal and probably has nothing to do with your latest tweak.

Join an AdSense forum, several if possible. Share your tips with other members. Discuss what works and what doesn't work for you. Every once in a while, a forum member might alert you to a possible violation of the AdSense TOS. It could be just a false alarm, but I prefer to be safe than sorry!

*When in doubt, dash an email to AdSense support, at: adsense-support@Google.com*

*Most emails are answered quickly by a real person. They won't suspend your account for asking them, but they might if you don't ask!*

Read all you can and jot down every good idea. It will keep your interest levels high and give you something new to work on all the time.

**Every new 'tweak' is your stepping stone to AdSense success.**

Once you've reached a certain level, it's easy to say 'Cool! I've figured it all out!' But take it from me — Internet Marketing keeps changing and the rules will change for you too.

Don't be like the two lazy little-people in "Who moved my cheese?" Keep looking for new ways to make money with AdSense. Replace ideas that no longer seem to work with new ideas and inspiration. Some people I know are still rubbing their backsides after the dot-com bust.

It's always easier when you see it coming, than when it takes you by surprise!

Remember the story about 'The Emperor's New Clothes'? There's a lesson in it for all of us Internet Marketers, and it's this:

It doesn't matter how much money you've made with AdSense or what the IQ tests say about you: **It isn't working till your stats say so!**

## 16.1 A Sample AdSense Journal

For example, let's say you have a website about Bonsai trees. You read this book and you decide to start implementing the strategies that I've been talking about.

Your original stats might look something like this. You print these out and use them for comparison:

| Date | Page Impressions | Clicks | Page CTR | Page eCPM | Your earnings |
|------|------------------|--------|----------|-----------|---------------|
| 5/1/05 | 8020 | 160 | 2.0% | 5.04 | 40.04 |
| 5/2/05 | 8186 | 172 | 2.1% | 5.53 | 45.27 |
| 5/3/05 | 8071 | 153 | 1.9% | 4.92 | 39.76 |
| 5/4/05 | 7792 | 156 | 2.0% | 5.50 | 42.89 |
| 5/5/05 | 6712 | 154 | 2.3% | 5.76 | 38.65 |
| 5/6/05 | 6596 | 132 | 2.0% | 5.70 | 37.65 |
| 5/7/05 | 7134 | 157 | 2.2% | 5.81 | 41.45 |

Clearly, your goal is going to be to lift up those CTRs, and by now you should have all sorts of ideas about how you're going to do that. You write down your first three:

- **3-Way Matching** — Text color, background and text size
- **Layout** — Moving ads above the fold where they'll be most prominent
- **Targeting ads** — Changing titles to improve relevancy and improving keywords

You're already using 336 x 280 ads so you decide to start with 3-Way Matching and change all your ads so that they blend in with your page. You make the background color of the ads match the background color of your site and the size and color of the ad text the same as the size and color of your body text.

A week later, your stats look like this:

| Date | Page Impressions | Clicks | Page CTR | Page eCPM | Your earnings |
|------|------------------|--------|----------|-----------|---------------|
| 5/8/05 | 8123 | 236 | 2.9% | 5.08 | 41.27 |
| 5/9/05 | 8135 | 244.05 | 3.0% | 6.02 | 48.97 |
| 5/10/05 | 8024 | 249 | 3.1% | 5.90 | 48.65 |
| 5/11/05 | 7926 | 238 | 3.0% | 5.92 | 46.93 |
| 5/12/05 | 7865 | 252 | 3.2% | 5.62 | 44.26 |
| 5/13/05 | 6645 | 193 | 2.9% | 6.10 | 40.52 |
| 5/14/05 | 7103 | 220 | 3.1% | 6.06 | 43.05 |

Already your weekly incomes have risen from $285.71 to $313.65 and your average CTR has gone up by a full percentage point. That's a good start, but you've still got a fair way to go.

You print out this week's report and write next to it "3-Way Matching" so that you know exactly what you did to create those changes. Now you know how much 3-Way Matching is worth to your incomes.

Next, you move the ads that you have at the bottom of your pages to the areas above the fold and place them in prominent positions. A week later, you print out the following stats:

| Date | Page Impressions | Clicks | Page CTR | Page eCPM | Your earnings |
|------|------------------|--------|----------|-----------|---------------|
| 5/15/05 | 8365 | 343 | 4.1% | 5.93 | 49.65 |
| 5/16/05 | 8296 | 324 | 3.9% | 6.04 | 50.09 |
| 5/17/05 | 8032 | 321 | 4.0% | 6.42 | 51.59 |
| 5/18/05 | 7920 | 317 | 4.0% | 6.30 | 49.93 |
| 5/19/05 | 7853 | 306 | 3.9% | 6.20 | 48.67 |
| 5/20/05 | 6725 | 282 | 4.2% | 6.68 | 44.92 |
| 5/21/05 | 7145 | 293 | 4.1% | 6.51 | 46.55 |

Again, your CTR has risen by another percentage point and your weekly income has gone up to $341.40. Next to this set of stats, you write "Layout" and you place them in your journal after your second set.

Now things are getting a little trickier. Your ads are blended onto the page and they're in prominent positions. But you find that they aren't always showing the most relevant ads. On your page on growing bonsai from cuttings for example, you find that you're getting lots of ads about scrap booking. A look at your server logs supports your hunch that these aren't getting any clicks at all. You create a channel for that page and follow your stats for a week. The original stats look like this:

| Channel | Ad Unit Impressions | Clicks | Ad Unit CTR | Ad Unit eCPM | Your earnings |
|---|---|---|---|---|---|
| Cuttings page | 829 | 8 | 1.0% | 1.44 | 1.20 |
| Cuttings page | 764 | 9 | 1.2% | 1.89 | 1.44 |
| Cuttings page | 801 | 7 | 0.9% | 1.22 | 0.98 |
| Cuttings page | 712 | 7 | 1.0% | 1.37 | 0.98 |
| Cuttings page | 758 | 10 | 1.3% | 1.85 | 1.40 |
| Cuttings page | 652 | 5 | 0.8% | 1.07 | 0.70 |
| Cuttings page | 704 | 6 | 0.9% | 1.19 | 0.84 |

That's pretty weak but as few of your users are likely to be interested in scrap booking, it's not too surprising. So you change the title of the page from *www.Bonsai.com/cuttings.html* to *www.Bonsai.com/tree_cuttings.html* and turn the word "cuttings" into "tree-cuttings", especially in the area beneath the ad box.

You upload, wait for the robot to index your page again and check that you're now getting ads from gardening and horticulture sites.

After a week, you find that your stats for that page look like this:

| Channel | Ad Unit Impressions | Clicks | Ad Unit CTR | Ad Unit eCPM | Your earnings |
|---|---|---|---|---|---|
| Cuttings page | 1300 | 52 | 4.0% | 6.40 | 8.32 |
| Cuttings page | 1423 | 58 | 4.1% | 6.52 | 9.28 |
| Cuttings page | 1346 | 52 | 3.9% | 6.18 | 8.32 |
| Cuttings page | 1256 | 50 | 3.9% | 6.40 | 8.04 |
| Cuttings page | 1156 | 44 | 3.8% | 6.09 | 7.04 |
| Cuttings page | 1098 | 45 | 4.0% | 6.56 | 7.20 |
| Cuttings page | 1247 | 49 | 3.9% | 6.29 | 7.84 |

Again, you'd want to print out this page and place it in your journal.

So far in the last three weeks, these simple tweaks would have already increased your weekly income by over $104.

*And there's still plenty more you can do!*

You can make sure that every page is optimized, you can look for higher-paying keywords and you can experiment with different colors and layouts, search boxes and multiple ads to increase your revenues.

And of course, you can create more pages and more sites.

Note that only in the last example (when you changed the keywords, improving your position in the search engines) did any of the changes affect your impressions. These tweaks simply made the most of the traffic you already have!

Of course, if you add more traffic, you'll make more money.

The important thing to remember is that you should be recording everything you do and keeping a close eye on the results. Within a few weeks, you'll have a complete record of all the changes you've made and what they're worth to your bottom line.

# CHAPTER
# 17

## Other Contextual
## Advertising Programs

# OTHER CONTEXTUAL ADVERTISING PROGRAMS

AdSense is probably the easiest way to generate revenue with your website — I know it's making me a fantastic amount of money — but it's certainly not the only way you can make money using contextualized advertising.

In this chapter, we're going to look at some of the other programs that you could use — either instead of AdSense or as well as AdSense. Just remember that Google's Terms of Service do not allow other context-driven advertising on the same page as their own program.

Let's start with advertising programs that work with AdSense.

## 17.1 Kontera — Making Your Words Pay

Kontera (*www.Kontera.com*) is a great way to make extra revenue. Instead of putting ad units on your site, like AdSense does, Kontera highlights particular keywords in your text and brings up an ad when the user mouses over.

The words are marked out from regular links by an underline and a second dotted line, and you can change the colors of the text, the background and the links.

*Fig. 17.1 Mousing over to bring up ads with Kontera at JoelComm.com.*

"I suspected that many media outlets would tilt to the left because surveys have shown that reporters tend to vote more Democrat than Republican," said Tim Groseclose, a UCLA p | Poll: Democrats Not Religion Friendly | was surprised at just how pronounc | Americans find Democratic party to be less religion friendly than before. A notable change from the past "Overall, | year. Read more. | ared to members of Congress | pewforum.org | bias in that nearly all of them lear | Advertisement          what's this? | sity of Missouri economist and public policy scholar.

I use Kontera on my personal blog at JoelComm.com and I've been pretty impressed with the results. The ads are fun to bring up, they're relevant and they're totally unobtrusive.

But like AdSense, you will need to play with them to maximize your revenues. There are so many different factors that affect your incomes with Kontera, such as which keywords you want high-lighted, where you want those words to appear on the page and which colors to choose for the best results, that it took me some time figure out all of the best combinations.

It also took me a few phone calls directly to the people who'd created it to get an idea of what happens behind the scenes of the program so that I can maximize my income.

Once I'd figured out all of those best strategies, I put them together in a short book so that other publishers can shorten their learning curve. You can find that book at *www.KonteraSecrets.com.*

If you're going to put Kontera on your site in addition to AdSense — and I can't think of a single reason why you shouldn't — you will need that book to shoot straight to the high revenues.

## 17.2 Chitika — All Malls, More Money

Kontera fits so neatly into your site, you'll hardly notice the difference to your page.

You will notice the difference in your revenues though.

Chitika's eMiniMalls are more intrusive than Kontera's text links but that's not necessarily a bad thing. One of their greatest advantages is that they are just so eye-catching and attractive.

The eMiniMalls are product ads that come with a number of tabs that can be selected just by mousing over. Those tabs include a list of Best Deals (with paid links to advertisers), a description of the product, reviews and a search box that draws on Chitika's catalog. Each ad also comes with a picture of the image.

If the ads are left contextualized, they can't be run together with AdSense. Turn off the contextualization though and you can choose the ads you serve yourself — and run them with AdSense.

That's a huge benefit: no more messing around with keywords or playing with text. You can just do a search, find an ad you like and start presenting it to your users.

Again, there are all sorts of factors involved in making eMiniMalls work at their best, from deciding which tabs to display (you can choose those too!) to figuring out how to use the ads together with ad units. There are some great ways to make them work together.

I've played around with these ads as well, come up with some very effective strategies and written them up as another book. You can find that volume at *www.ChitikaSecrets.com.*

*Fig. 17.2 A Chitika eMiniMall. Tempted?*

## 17.3 ContextCASH — Affiliate Revenue The Easy Way

ContextCASH (*www.ContextCash.com*) looks pretty similar to Kontera but it works in a very different way. You still get the highlighted words that appear in your text but instead of bringing up an ad when you mouse over, these links lead directly to affiliate sites.

Again, the links are unobtrusive, they don't clash with your ad units and they're compatible with AdSense.

And they can bring in good money too.

If you're looking to really broaden your revenue base by adding affiliate links in addition to your pay-per-click and CPM ads, then ContextCASH is a great option.

*Fig. 17.3 Your affiliate links scattered across the page and boosting your AdSense earnings with ContextCASH.*

All of these programs work with AdSense. I think it's pretty unlikely that they'll give you more money than AdSense but they can be very useful ways to bring in a little extra income.

Let's talk now about programs that aren't compatible with AdSense...

## 17.4 Yahoo! Publisher Network

Yahoo! Publisher Network (YPN) (*http://publisher.yahoo.com/*) is probably the number one competitor to Google. In fact, they pretty much copied what AdSense had done... but didn't do it quite as well.

On the plus-side, their ad formats are largely the same. So if you need to switch from AdSense to YPN, you should be able to keep the exact same optimization, at least as regards how the ads looks (although YPN doesn't have Ad Links or Search, so you'd lose those.)

They also have ads in RSS which could bring in some extra revenues if you're using that on your site.

As to which ads you get served though, that's a whole other ball game. One of the biggest problems with YPN is that the first ads they serve are often Run-Of-The-Network (RON) ads, Yahoo!'s answer to

public service ads. These are just ads for companies that seem to have struck a special deal with YPN.

They pay well when you get a click out of them, but they're not contextualized so you don't get many clicks. They occur much more frequently that public service ads and they're much harder to get rid of.

And there are no CPM ads on Yahoo!, which can be a good thing or a bad thing depending on the size of your site and your experience.

Most publishers find that they get better results with AdSense than they do with YPN... although we all keep a close eye on YPN to see if they improve enough to attract us.

## 17.5 AdBrite

Google's big thing is serving contextual ads. Their program checks the content of your site and delivers ads that they think your users will like. AdBrite is much simpler.

The idea behind AdSense is that people tend to ask popular sites to advertise their links. You've probably had that happen to you. Instead of asking for a link in return though, you could ask for money.

AdBrite is a clearing house for sites that want to sell advertising space on their pages and for advertisers who want to choose where they want to place their ads.

For advertisers, the advantage over Google is that they know exactly where their ads are appearing and for exactly how much money each time.

Publishers — like you — get to set your own ad rates, and you have the right to approve or reject every ad before it's placed on your site. That gives you the power to choose your ads and your price instead of relying on whatever Google give you.

Those are the advantages. The disadvantages are that it's just not in the same league as AdSense... or YPN.

You can learn more about AdBrite at *www.AdBrite.com*.

## 17.6 Kanoodle — Bright Ads

The same criticism can be made of Kanoodle's BrightAds service, which is similar to Google's. It's a search engine that delivers contextual ads to publishers' websites.

The contextualizing isn't quite as accurate as Google's but BrightAds does offer a number of options that Google doesn't offer — or at least not yet. Its RSS advertising program has been around for a while, it has a focus on local sites which might be attractive to businesses with local markets (or sites with content of local interest) and it also serves ads related to previous user behavior. If a user visits a lot of real estate sites, for example he could continue to receive ads about real estate even if he's on a site about sports. That means your site could be displaying ads that have nothing to do with your content.

That's all creative stuff and it's nice to see new ideas. It would be nicer though to see revenues that compete with Google's and I haven't heard of anyone earning more with BrightAds than they can earn with Google.

BrightAds might be worth looking at if you want to make money with your RSS feed but I'm not convinced they're going to give Google or Yahoo! any worries. Learn more about Kanoodle's BrightAds at *www.Kanoodle.com/about/brightads.cool*.

## 17.7  Searchfeed

Searchfeed is slightly better, especially for international publishers. It also supplies contextualized ads to advertisers but offers geotargeting services which gives them a wide global reach, useful if you're based outside the United States.

You can integrate the ads smoothly into your site, either by cutting and pasting the HTML from their site or even by asking their own specialists to help you increase your CTR. And they have a good reputation for paying on time.

Whether they'll give you more money than Google is a different question though. The only way to find that out is to try it but if you find that you're doing well with Google, then why would you bother?

If, for some reason, you don't want to use Google — or can't use Google — and YPN isn't your cup of tea either, then you might find Searchfeed a good alternative.

You can learn more about Searchfeed at *www.SearchFeed.com*.

# CHAPTER
# 18

# Getting Traffic To
# Your Web Site

# GETTING TRAFFIC TO YOUR WEB SITE

One of the most frequent questions I am asked is "Will your ebook teach me how to get more traffic to my web site?" Lots of people have written books — and series of books — on generating traffic. The focus of *this* book is to show you how to maximize the traffic that you already have. And while tips for building pages through forums and free content are excellent ideas, they are no replacement for a solid course on how to get more people to visit your site. Because this question is so common though, I will address it briefly in this chapter. I'll give you the basics, describe some unusual ideas that some people are using and tell you where you can get all the information you need.

In the next chapter, you'll also find a quick run-through of search engine optimization.

## 18.1 Advertising

Let's start with the obvious: buying advertising. We've already talked about AdWords/AdSense arbitrage but exactly the same principle applies to buying your traffic from other sources too.

For example, the minimum price for advertising at Overture is ten cents per click and you must spend at least $20 each month. If you can see that the ads being served on your site are generating less than ten cents per click then you're never going to make a profit.

Exactly the same is true of any other pay-per-click advertising campaign.

One of the advantages of following your AdSense stats is that you can estimate how much the clicks on your ads are worth. That can tell you how much you can afford to pay for clicks from other sites when you buy advertising.

It might well pay to advertise, but before you buy make sure it pays a profit.

## 18.2 Reciprocal Linking

Many people focus on linking in order to improve their search engine rankings. That's important but don't forget that the links themselves can be one of your biggest sources of traffic!

Probably the easiest way to invite links (apart from searching out related sites and writing to each one) is to add a "link" section to your pages where webmasters can choose a banner, button or text link to place on their site. On the same page, they can also submit their own site for linking. That should help you swap links without being swamped by sites looking for free placement.

The most critical factor when requesting a link though is where the site places it. Links on the home page always do better than a link buried on one of the internal pages and a good banner or graphic link on a site with content related to yours will usually get more clicks than a text link.

If you find that your links aren't appearing on the pages you want, there are a couple of simple remedies that you can use.

The first is to ask for a better position! If you have a good relationship with the webmaster or if it's a small site, there's a good chance that they'll agree. It certainly won't hurt to ask.

Not everyone is so generous though, and another option is to offer something in return. A link in a similar position on your own site can make a good deal if your sites are of similar size but you can also offer content or even a special page for that site's users.

If you have a site about furniture for example, and you want a link at a top directory for home furnishings then you could create a special

welcome page for users of that site to draw them deeper into yours and deliver targeted ads. You might even want to go as far as creating a sort of co-branded version of your site for their users to click into. As long as you're getting paid when the users click on the ads, what do you care whose design they're looking at?

## 18.3 Send A Friend

There's nothing like viral marketing to promote your site! It's free, it comes with trusted recommendations and it gives you great CTR.

Each of your content pages should have a link marked "Send a friend" which opens a form so that the user can send your URL onwards. Until Google allows ads in email, there's little point in AdSense members sending actual content but there's no reason why you (or your users) can't send links to pages with ads.

## 18.4 Offline Marketing

One of the biggest mistakes that people make when they build an Internet business is to forget that there's a world outside the Internet! Just because you make money out of traffic doesn't mean you have to source all of that traffic online.

You should make sure that your URL is listed on all of your marketing material: your business cards, Yellow Pages ads, flyers, envelopes, freebies and just about anything else you can think of.

You should certainly have your site address in your email signatures.

## 18.5 Promoting Your Blog

I've talked quite a bit about blogging in this book, mostly because I know from experience that it's possible to make a very nice income from a good blog but also because a lot of people aren't making the most of the blogs they have.

If you've got AdSense on your blog, there's a whole range of different things that you can easily do to increase your traffic and earn extra cash.

The first thing you should do is make sure that your blog is set to ping rpc.pingomatic.com as soon you've updated. *Pingomatic.com* offers a free all-in-one pinging service that covers all the large blog directories and search engines. On Blogger.com, you can find this in your settings; other blog tools, such as Movable Type and Wordpress have a similar option.

You should also set up an RSS feed to let people know when you update. Apart from the fact that you can now place ads on your feeds, it will also keep your regular users coming back to see more ads (and to see your latest posts).

Instead of linking to the previous month's or the previous week's posts, each page should also have its own link. Sounds obvious, right? And yet how many blogs have you seen with one link to about twenty different entries? One link per entry means more pages for ads, better links from external sites and higher search engine rankings.

You should certainly comment on other people's blogs, especially those that write about the same sort of things as your site, but ultimately the best way to get traffic to your blog is to make it good. If your writing is dull or difficult to read, it doesn't matter how hard you push it, no one will want to read it — and those who do stay won't stick around to click the ads.

## 18.6 Public Relations And Publicity

Just about all of the methods that you use to bring people to your site will cost you money. You'll have to pay for ads on other sites, you'll have to give up valuable real estate on your site to lists of links and you'll have to decide how much you want to pay for an AdWords campaign or to get yourself promoted through Overture.

Publicity can be free.

It doesn't have to be of course. You can pay a PR expert to publicize your site for you and place articles in the press on your behalf... but it's not necessary and they can be too expensive for most sites, especially at the beginning.

Or you can simply create a good quality press release yourself, fax it out to the media and wait for reporters to call.

Sound difficult?

It really isn't. A press release is just one page and will take between twenty and forty minutes to write.

There are a number of rules you have to follow: you need a gripping headline; you have to include a quote; and you have to be available for the interview to name just three. Most importantly though you have to have a story the press want to run.

Telling them that you've just launched a new site isn't going to cut it. Telling them that your new site is going to set a new trend or change some people's lives just might.

Think about the effect that your piece of "news" will have on the public and you've got the beginnings of a great story.

And what do you get in return for doing that? Well, not only do you get the name of your business in the press, you also get the halo that comes with it. When you're in the media, people assume that you're an expert. You become the number one source for whatever your website offers.

And to underline that fact, you can even put a button on your home page that says something like: "As Seen On CNN!"

Sound good?

The real expert on marketing through free publicity is Paul Hartunian. This is the guy who bought a hunk of wood that had been cut from the Brooklyn Bridge during renovations, cut it into one-inch cubes and wrote a press release with the headline "New Jersey Man Sells Brooklyn Bridge For $19.95".

He was on CNN for two days and the story was run as far away as Peru.

He now lives on a 30-acre estate and teaches people how to use publicity for their businesses. You can order his publicity kit at *www.Hartunian.com*.

## 18.7 Learn From A Pro

Do you know John Reese? If not, you probably haven't spent much time in Internet marketing circles. John is the leading guru for teaching people how to get more traffic to their web site(s). He leads special multi-day seminars to small groups, charging up to $5000/person to attend. And you know what? His students walk away feeling that they got a BARGAIN!

John has now made his marketing course available to the general public at a FRACTION of the cost. It's full of DVDs, audio CDs, textbooks, workbooks and tip sheets to help you build a comprehensive Internet marketing strategy.

I own a copy of John's *Traffic Secrets* and am pleased to give it my very personal endorsement. While I could attempt to teach you everything I know about Internet marketing, there is no point in attempting to reinvent the wheel. Everything you need to know is in this is course, and the investment is very minor for people who intend to build a successful Internet business that will last.

If you want to read more about John's Traffic Secrets course, go to: *www.Adsense-Secrets.com/trafficsecrets.html*.

# CHAPTER
# 19

# Search Engine
# Optimization

# SEARCH ENGINE OPTIMIZATION

In the previous chapter, I talked about a number of different ways that you can increase your traffic. Probably the most important method though is to get a high ranking on search engines. That's free traffic.

Again, there are all sorts of books and experts who can help you improve your SEO and win a top spot at a site. I have had experience with a number of strategies that could help you improve your ranking. I'd like to share them with you now.

## 19.1 Robot.txt

The first thing you need to know about indexing your site at search engines is that you control which pages are indexed and which are excluded. You do that with a file called robots.txt.

Robots.txt contains nothing more than a record of which robots should index which pages.

Without going into too much detail, there are two conventions used in a robots.txt file:

> User-agent: [Defines which robots the site is addressing.]
>
> Disallow: [Allows you to list the sites or robots you want to exclude.]

In general, you're probably going to use "User-agent: *" to make sure that you're addressing the robots of every search engine and you'll probably want include all of your pages (although you might want to exclude your directories: "Disallow: /cgi-bin/").

Robots.txt just allows you to control which robots index which pages. It's important to have in your directory but it won't really increase your search engine rankings.

Titles, URL's and links are much more important.

## 19.2  Titles And URLs

I mentioned earlier that Metatags just aren't what they used to be. I also said that it's important that your titles and URLs contain the most important keywords for each of your pages in order to keep the ads relevant.

But those titles and URLs don't just influence your ads; they also affect your search engine rankings.

A page about toy cars called cars.html might have a low ranking when someone looks for information about cars. Change the name to toy_cars.html and you should get a much higher ranking when someone looks for "toy cars".

The more relevant your URL is and the easier it is to read, the better. www.domain.com/page is always an improvement over http://domain.com/page.php?newsid=1234583373. That is why on my website *www.familyfirst.com*, I use URL's like *www.familyfirst.com/miss_abigails_time_warp.html* rather than strings of number which confuse the robots.

One of the first places you should look when you want to improve your rankings is your titles and URLs.

## 19.3 Links

The more links you have, the better — And the better the sites that list those links the more they'll be worth.

It's one thing to swap links and ask for links but it is worth aiming to put your links on sites that look good and have high rankings. In fact, being listed on a poor site can bring your ranking down.

One of the best places to place links to improve your search engine rankings is on forums. Add a comment and include your URL in your signature. Google's spiders love forums and review them every week. And because these sites tend have quite high ranking, those posts will do wonders for your listings.

You can also buy links on sites like *www.Adzaar.com*, *www.AdBrite.com*, and *www.LinkAdage.com*. These allow you to choose sites on which you can place your own links.

On my own site *www.BuyJoelDessert.com*, for example, I give page links to people who satisfy my sweet tooth with a donation to my cause. (I'm still hungry by the way, so feel free to sign up and make my dentist happy!)

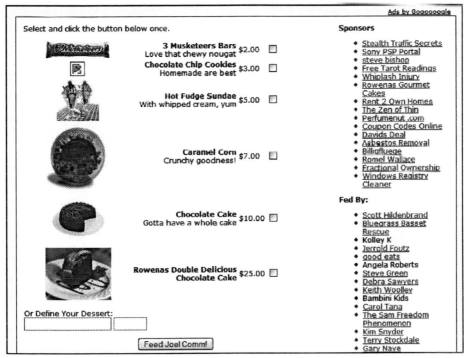

*Fig. 19.1 Links for sale on BuyJoelDessert.com.*

I know of several associates who have done something similar, allowing their visitors a tangible way to say "thank you" for their online efforts.

Smart site owners see opportunity in this strategy as you can acquire quality links rather inexpensively. Here are some additional examples:

*www.BuyLeoALatte.com*

*www.BuyBarbaraCoffee.com*

You can actually acquire the "Buy Me A Drink" script that all these sites run off of at *jcomm.delavera.hop.clickbank.net.*

## 19.4 Create Gateways

Usually, your links will lead directly to your home page. That's where you see your site as starting and that's where you want them to enter.

But if the content the user wants to see is on one of the internal pages, there's no reason for them to have to click around to find it. Fill that page with keywords that relate to the content on that page and it will have its own search engine ranking — and well-targeted ads.

So if you have a site about cats and one of your pages was about cat food, it would make sense to put plenty of cat food keywords on the page. That would get you cat food ads and a high ranking on search engines when someone does a search for "cat food" rather than just people who wanted to know about "cats."

## 19.5 Automatic Submissions

Submitting your site to all of the search engines from Google and Yahoo! right down to the smallest ones, and optimizing each of your pages for high ranking can be a drag. You also have to keep submitting the site on a regular basis and constantly check your position if you want to keep it.

The search engines are always re-indexing and reorganizing. A site that can be in the top spot one week can be a couple of pages over a week later. (Good news if you're low down, not so good if you've spent hours changing your pages to climb the rankings.)

That's why many webmasters simply outsource their SEO so that they can concentrate on content.

There are lots of companies that do this. Search Engine Blaster for example, lets you choose from over 600,000 engines but there are plenty of others.

Personally, I think that's a bit of a waste of time. Only Google, Yahoo and MSN are important, in that order.

## 19.6 SEO Tools

There are a number of tools that I recommend to help with search engine optimization. The first is the Google Toolbar, which will let you keep track of your page ranking. You can download it for free at *Toolbar.Google.com/googlebar.html.*

*Fig. 19.2 The Google Toolbar: Pretty and useful too.*

The Alexa toolbar is also useful and will show you how your site ranks against others. You can download the Alexa toolbar at *Pages.Alexa.com/prod_serv/quicktour.html.*

*Fig. 19.3 The Alexa Toolbar: Is your site number one yet?*

### SEO Elite

SEO Elite is a really excellent tool for learning from your most successful competitors. You can discover the optimum number of times to repeat keywords, where you should put them, whether or not to use h1 and h2 tags and even your competitors' link strategies, and a huge amount more.

In short, you can find out exactly how your competitors have got to the top of the search engines, learn what they did — and do the exact same thing to swipe their spot.

You can learn more about SEO Elite and pick up your copy from *www.Adsense-Secrets.com/seoelite.html*.

## Reciprocal Manager

Reciprocal Manager takes much of the headache out of managing your links. As you continue to optimize your site, you will find yourself winning more links on other sites and being asked to host links from other site. Reciprocal Manager creates a professional-looking, neatly organized links directory that's good for both your link partners and your visitors.

The program also lets you offer sites the option of placing their links on more than one site at the same time and, most importantly, to search for other sites to link to based on search word or phrase.

Learn more about Reciprocal Manager at *wwwAdsense-Secrets.com/reciprocalmanager.html*.

## Stomping The Search Engines

Finally, Brad Fallon is one of the biggest experts when it comes to SEO optimization. His wedding favors site grossed over $1,000,000 within a short time of launching, mainly due to his ability to get his site prime placement in Google and the other search engines.

I've met Brad and chatted to him about his SEO optimization and I can tell you, he knows his stuff! I thought I knew a bunch about SEO, but after spending a couple of hours with Brad, I feel like a novice.

You can have thousands of web pages, but without a great search engine optimization plan, you many not be making the money you want to with AdSense. I HIGHLY recommend picking up Brad Fallon's 10 audio CD series, Stomping the Search Engines.

It is over 8 hours of Brad's teaching on how to duplicate his success for your web site(s).

I own the set and recommend it wholeheartedly. It is truly FULL of incredible material that you will find very useful to helping you reach your goals.

To read more about Stomping the Search Engines and acquire your own copy at *www.Adsense-Secrets.com/seoexpert.html.*

## 19.7 A Word About Cloaking

One issue that surfaced recently in the contextualized advertising world is "cloaking": presenting a different site to the Google bot than the one you present to users.

There can be good reasons for doing this. If you've got a forum for example, the bot could read all the information on your page related to forums, links and the design etc., find that it outweighs your forum content and serve you ads related to forums in general instead of your site in particular.

You could also find that your search engine listings are affected too: instead of appearing nice and high on the results page following a search for your topic, you might only appear to people looking for forums. That's not likely to win you much traffic.

One solution is to strip the site down using javascript or one of the tools available online so that when the Google bot comes, it only reads the content.

Of course, you could also fool the bot into thinking that your site is about... well, anything really. You could spam Google into showing your site to anyone who was searching for anything.

**And that's why Google banned the practice altogether.**

Any form of cloaking, whether it's to get better targeted ads, improve your search engine rankings... or spam the search engines is a breach of Google's TOS and could get you banned.

So what should you do if you find that your design has a bigger influence on your ads and ranking than your content?

The best — and simplest thing to do — is to make sure that the description and keyword meta tags are all filled in properly with terms relevant to your content.

Section Targeting can de-emphasize problematic areas of your website and might well affect your search engine rankings (it's certainly worth a try).

And if these don't solve your problem, you might want to think of a redesign.

# CHAPTER

# 20

## AdSense No-Nos

# ADSENSE NO-NOS

Google is very protective of its AdSense program and is a pretty strict ad provider. It has a relatively long page of Terms and Conditions (*www.Google.com/adsense/terms*) and monitors sites pretty closely. While YPN usually sends a warning to sites that it believes have broken its terms and conditions, Google has been known to cut people off right away.

And that can be pretty painful.

I do recommend that you read the AdSense Terms and Conditions. I realize that they're not much fun and they're hardly a gripping read, but they are important, especially when you start really pushing your ads to their limits. To make it easier for you though, I've gone through those terms and pulled out the most important restrictions contained in them.

This list is not a replacement for reading the Terms page — you're still going to have to do that. They just might make it clearer so that you're less likely to make a very costly mistake.

- **One individual or entity cannot hold more than one AdSense account; all accounts will be closed**.

  This is important if you have many sites covering different topics and are worried about the effects of Smart Pricing. You might want to open a separate account in a spouse's name or open more than one business.

- **You cannot modify the JavaScript or other code provided in any way**.

  Google is pretty strict about this. Cut into the code and you risk the axe.

- **Web pages cannot contain solely ads, a Search Box or a referral button.**

  Blank pages with nothing more than AdSense ads are pretty rare; pages which contain only ads of different types are much more common. Google is working against these sorts of things and you'll probably find yourself if not banned, then almost certainly Smart Priced out.

- **Ads cannot appear on pages that are "under construction," used for registration, chat, contain adult, objectionable or illegal content. And they can't be used in emails either.**

  If you have a site that's in any way morally objectionable, then AdSense isn't for you. That's the bottom line.

  More relevant for most people though is the idea that you can't put AdSense on every page of a website. There are all sorts of pages on many people's sites that really don't contain any content, like password pages or error messages. You can't use them as places to put ads.

- **You cannot generate searches, clicks or impressions by any method other than genuine user interest.**

  So no automatic bots or clicking your own ads or any of that nonsense. That's just fraud and Google will spot it in a second.

- **You cannot display anything on your Web page that could be confused as an AdSense ad.**

  That's an interesting rule that prevents people from putting up affiliate links that look like ad units to try to cash in on Google's brand. In theory, this rule could cause a problem for someone who blended the ads into the page by making link lists that looked similar to ad units. As long as those links aren't ads though, and as long as you don't write "Ads by Goooogle" on them, I doubt if Google would have a problem with them.

- **You cannot place any other contextualized ads on a page with AdSense.**

  So it's either AdSense or YPN, not both.

- **If you're using a Google Search box, you cannot use any other search service on the page.**

  Again, Google wants a monopoly of services on your site. You can't offer your users the option of searching through Google or Yahoo; it's either-or, not both-and.

- **You cannot put anything between the ad link and the ad site.**

  So if you were thinking of trying to capture your lost traffic by redirecting ad clicks to another of your sites, think again. But who thinks of that?

- **You cannot communicate advertisers directly concerning the ads on your site.**

  That would have been quite useful. You could have written to an advertiser and suggested ways in which they could make their copy more effective for your users.

  Of course, you could also suggest they advertise directly on your site and cut out the Google middleman...

  Interestingly though, you can do all of this on your "Advertise on this site" landing page.

- **You cannot change the order of the information in an ad unit.**

  This is pretty well covered by the ban on changing the code. But again, it might have been nice to put the ads that are most likely to get the most clicks at the top of the list, even if they pay less.

  But putting the ones with the highest bid price there though isn't a bad idea either.

- **You cannot reveal your click-through rates or any other information about your site performance.**

Which is why I haven't quoted my own CTR figures in this book. But you can reveal the amount of Google's gross payments to you, which I have done.

These rules are all pretty straightforward and for the most part, easy to follow. Usually, if someone has been banned from AdSense it's because they've clicked on their own ads and Google didn't believe that it was an accident. That's just rotten luck.

## 20.1 What To Do If Your AdSense Account Gets Closed

So what should you do if you get that dreaded email from AdSense informing you that your account has been shut down?

Well, the first thing to remember is that you've pretty much got no power at all. Google's Terms make it very clear that they have the right to kick someone out of their program whenever they feel like it and there's no court of appeal.

But Google aren't a nasty bunch and they will listen to you if you feel you've been hard done by. Your first step then should be to send them an email asking why you've been banned and explaining that your click was accidental.

Usually, as long as you're telling the truth and there weren't too many clicks, you should be fine. Similarly, if you know you've clicked on your own ads — or if you know that someone else has been clicking on your ads (that can happen too sometimes) — you should drop Google a line immediately. You'll lose the value of those clicks, but at least you'll keep your account open.

And if all else fails and you find yourself cut off, there's always Yahoo! Publisher Network combined with Chitika and Kontera ads.

It's unlikely you'll make as much as you did with AdSense, but you will still make something.

# CHAPTER 21

# Staying Up To Date And Learning The Latest AdSense Tips

# STAYING UP TO DATE AND LEARNING THE LATEST ADSENSE TIPS

AdSense changes all the time and lots of people are following those changes. They're talking about what those changes mean for publishers and how you can take advantage of them.

They're also discussing the new contextualized advertising systems that appear from time to time and commenting on how well they work.

Most serious publishers pay close attention to these blogs and other sites. They're an invaluable source of first-hand information from people who have been there and done that. They'll save you a huge amount of time — and money.

I've put a short list of some of the most important sites to look at below. This isn't meant to be a complete list — that would be way too long — but these are a good place to start. They'll keep you in the loop and make sure your questions get answered.

- **www.JenSense.com**

  Jen's contextual advertising blog is a great read. She's always coming up with useful information and sometimes manages to dig up a real scoop (like what lies behind Smart Pricing). This should definitely be in your favorites.

- **www.ProBlogger.net**

  Darren is a blogger making a healthy six-figure income with his online thoughts and his advice about how to do the same thing. If you're running a blog, you really need to be reading it... and if you're not running a blog, you'll still find enough great advice to keep you busy too.

- **www.AssociatePrograms.com/discus/index.php**

Forums are a really great place to swap ideas and most importantly, ask questions. Publishers who are old hands at making serious money with AdSense are usually more than happy to share their knowledge. The forum at Associate Programs is a great place to pick up tips about everything from links to marketing.

- **Forums.DigitalPoint.com**

And the forums at Digital Point are at least as good, if not better, with plenty of information on AdSense.

- **www.AdSenseChat.com**

Finally, there's my own forum. You'll find plenty of people here swapping advice and sharing news about AdSense and other contextualized advertising systems... including me.

It's free to join, so I'll hope to see you there soon!

# CHAPTER
# 22

## Case Studies

# ⸬ CASE STUDIES ⸬

Throughout this book, I've been explaining all the different ways that you can optimize your site and boost your revenues. In this chapter, I've collected some examples.

All of these are real sites that employed the techniques that I describe in this book to make more money. I'll talk you through them so that you can see exactly what they did, why they did it — and do the same.

## 22.1 Freeafterrebate.info — Unmissable Ads

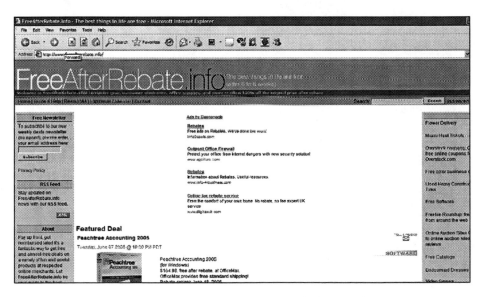

Fig. 22.1  Freeafterrebate.info puts its ads front and center.

It can take some courage to make your ads the most important thing the user sees when he looks at the page, but that's the approach that Freeafterrebate.info takes.

You can't miss these ads! They're right above the fold and slap-bang in the middle. This site saw a HUGE increase in revenue when they put their ads here.

And those links on the right? They're Adbrite links. Take a look at *www.FreeAfterRebate.info.*

## 22.2 Great Ideas For Integration From The Idea Box

*Fig. 22.2 Above the fold at Idea Box.*

Few sites do a better job of integrating their ads with the text as *TheIdeasBox.com* does.

Above the fold, there's a search box in the middle and an Ad Link unit on the left, beautifully blended into the site design so that you see it without noticing it's an ad.

Below the fold, just look how the ads slip into the links with 3-Way Matching. Perfect! Take a look at:

*Ideas.TheIdeaBox.com/ib.php?web=ideasbytype&type=Craft*

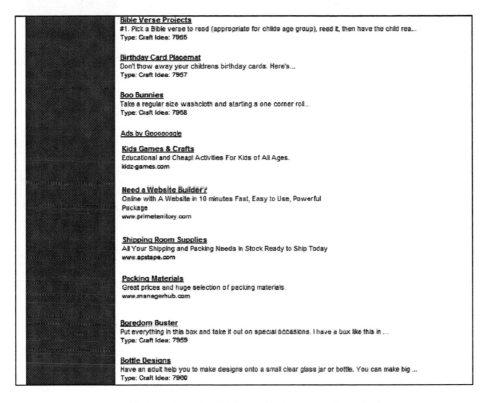

*Fig. 22.3 Below the fold: perfectly camouflaged ads.*

## 22.3  Gifts-911.com Gets Emergency Treatment With Multiple Ad Units

The most Adriana Copaceanu's site Gifts-911.com had made in one month was $31.19 — not much more than a dollar a day. She put a main ad unit above the fold, a second unit at the bottom of the page and an Ad Link unit on the right.

*Fig. 22.4 Gift-911.com gives its own revenues some first aid above the fold...*

After making the ads more prominent and adding more of them, revenues doubled the following the months and reached as high as $200 in the month after that!

Could Adriana do more?

Probably.

But this is a pretty good start!

Check out Gift-911.com at *www.Gift-911.com.*

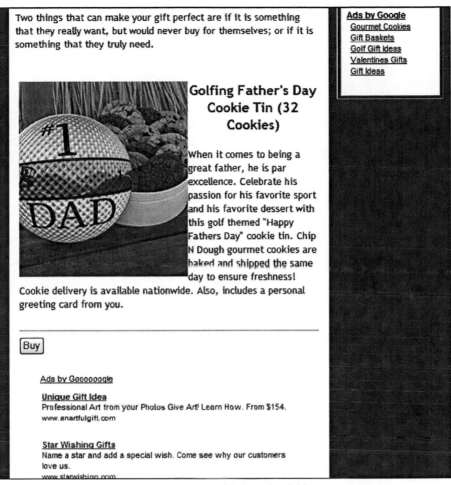

Two things that can make your gift perfect are if it is something that they really want, but would never buy for themselves; or if it is something that they truly need.

### Golfing Father's Day Cookie Tin (32 Cookies)

When it comes to being a great father, he is par excellence. Celebrate his passion for his favorite sport and his favorite dessert with this golf themed "Happy Fathers Day" cookie tin. Chip N Dough gourmet cookies are baked and shipped the same day to ensure freshness! Cookie delivery is available nationwide. Also, includes a personal greeting card from you.

Buy

*Fig. 22.5 ...and below the fold.*

## 22.4 StellaAwards — A Prize Winning Design

Success with AdSense is really all about making your ads blend in. *www.StellaAwards.com* have used a special design that aims to replicate a legal document. The ads on the right complement the text in the top right-hand corner — and led to almost 20 times more clicks overnight with that one simple improvement!

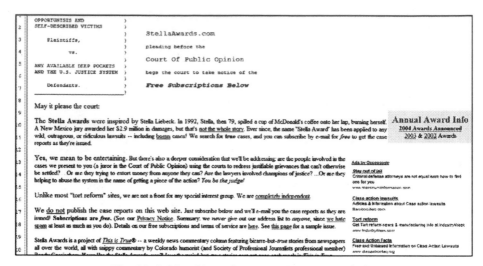

*Fig. 22.6  Matching ad; twenty times more clicks.*

# CONCLUSION

Do you see the power of the AdSense Code now?

Knowing the secrets of the AdSense Code can give you huge amounts of money. It can pay your mortgage, make your car payments and send you on the sort of vacations you've only dreamed of. If you want, it can even let you give up the day job and look forward to a life of working at home in your pajamas with no boss other than yourself.

Or it can give you enough money to buy a couple of candy bars each week.

The secret of AdSense success isn't complicated. You don't have to spend years in a classroom learning a new skill or head out to get a diploma. The principle is very basic:

*Serve interesting ads to users in a way that makes them want to click.*

You do that with layout. You do that by choosing the right size of ads. And you do it by blending the ad into the page.

Choosing the right keywords is important too, and so is bringing traffic to your site at a low price before selling them on to advertisers for a higher one.

Most important though is to keep a close eye on the results of everything you do so that you can see what works and what doesn't.

In this book, I've told you everything you need to know to supercharge your AdSense earnings. I've revealed all the secrets of the AdSense Code that have been uncovered so far. Apply the techniques I've described here, track the results and you should see your incomes rise as quickly as mine did!

If you want to go deeper in AdSense, you will want to visit *www.TheAdsenseCode.com* for additional information on continuing education.

And finally, if you've enjoyed this book and seen your revenues rise after implementing the strategies I recommend, you can pass on the word — and get paid for it.

You can find information about my affiliate program at *www.TheAdsenseCode.com/affiliates.html.*

Here's to your AdSense success!

I regularly receive email from readers. Everyone is so excited when they apply my tips and see their AdSense revenue increase! Here are a few emails and comment I received recently.

"I hate 'Get Rich Quick' schemes — but by doing the 'quick' items covered in his book, I quadrupled my daily earning average. Yes, you read that right. My income went up four times!"

~Raymond Camden

(*www.FusionAuthority.com/Reviews/Article.cfm/ArticleID:4509*)

"I don't know if you remember me but I was the "skeptic" that purchased your book a month ago. I wanted to give you an update on the results of implementing some of the changes you recommended. In the month since Owning AdSense Secrets, my click-through rate has more than TRIPLED and my daily earnings have QUADRUPLED, just like the calculator on your page said! Thank you SO much!"

~Name withheld by request

"I purchased your eBook yesterday. By 2:30 this afternoon I've already generated TWICE my average daily AdSense revenue. Although I've only implemented the first step recommended in your book, it looks like I've already tripled my AdSense income. Thank you!"

~Kenn Nesbit

"I just wanted to tell you that I have tripled my stats after buying your ebook!"

~Shawn Mcgarvey

"I really am benefiting from buying your book! My AdSense click-through rates have increased 100% within a week of using the tips and tricks from your book! I have already made my money back that I invested in your book. As a result I am presently making more money with AdSense on a daily basis than ever before. Thank you for sharing your insights."

~Kamau Austin

"Joel, I bought your e-book, and immediately tried some of your suggestions. (From the time I started reading it, I couldn't put it down until I was done.) To say my results were exciting is putting it mildly. We made over $500 in March on numbers that are still climbing! I've never written a referral letter before, but your book was such an excellent value I felt obligated."

~Chris Bartram

"Just writing to say "THANK YOU" for your wonderful ebook. I've increased my AdSense income by almost 300%, by applying your tips."

~Bingwen Lu

**CONCLUSION**     **227**

"I'm flat EXCITED about your book. I just downloaded it late last week, read it on Saturday, and started making your recommended changes in my AdSense Ads and some of the design on some of my sites to make the ads look less like ads. Unbelievable, but after only one day of changes on three of my sites, my click-through ratios have nearly tripled today! I have printed and read your book three times and plan to tell all of my clients about it."

~Ed Hudson

I love to receive email like this and I hope you will take the time to write me and share your AdSense success story! You may send me email at *Joel.Comm@Adsense-Secrets.com* or call My toll-free testimonial recording line at 1-800-609-9006 x9257. International callers may use 678-255-2174.

May your Google AdSense revenues multiply! (That makes Google AND You happy!)

# FREE ADSENSE CASE STUDIES REPORT AND RESOURCE PAGE FOR OUR READERS

This book contains many links to sites that I have used as examples, as well as a number of recommend resources and tools. Since I haven't found a way to be able to click a hyperlink in a printed book and have a web site appear, I have created a special resource page containing all links presented in this book. Point your web browser to:

## http://www.TheAdsenseCode.com/register.html

and provide your name and email address.

Here's what happens when you register your copy of *The AdSense Code*:

1) You will have instant access to a **members-only resource page** containing every link from this book categorized by chapter.

2) You will be eligible to receive my **free AdSense Secrets newsletter**, featuring the latest AdSense news and money-making strategies.

3) I will provide you with a **FREE AdSense Case Studies report** in digital form. This 30-page document contains more examples of how to do, and how NOT to do, AdSense! You will be able to instantly download this special report as my gift to you.

Be sure to bookmark the members link page that I send you! Occasionally site urls change, so please send me an email at *Joel.Comm@Adsense-Secrets.com* if you encounter a bad link.

# LEGALESE

Every effort has been made to accurately represent this product and it's potential. Even though this industry is one of the few where one can write their own check in terms of earnings, there is no guarantee that you will earn any money using the techniques and ideas in these materials. Examples in these materials are not to be interpreted as a promise or guarantee of earnings. Earning potential is entirely dependent on the person using our product, ideas and techniques. We do not purport this as a "get rich scheme."

Your level of success in attaining the results claimed in our materials depends on the time you devote to the program, ideas and techniques mentioned your finances, knowledge and various skills. Since these factors differ according to individuals, we cannot guarantee your success or income level. Nor are we responsible for any of your actions.

Materials in our product and our website may contain information that includes or is based upon forward-looking statements within the meaning of the securities litigation reform act of 1995. Forward-looking statements give our expectations or forecasts of future events. You can identify these statements by the fact that they do not relate strictly to historical or current facts. They use words such as "anticipate," "estimate," "expect," "project," "intend," "plan," "believe," and other words and terms of similar meaning in connection with a description of potential earnings or financial performance.

Any and all forward looking statements here or on any of our sales material are intended to express our opinion of earnings potential. Many factors will be important in determining your actual results and no guarantees are made that you will achieve results similar to ours or anybody else's, in fact no guarantees are made that you will achieve any results from our ideas and techniques in our material.

Results may vary, as with any business opportunity, you could make more or less. Success in ANY business opportunity is a result of hard work, time and a variety of other factors. No express or implied guarantees of income are made when purchasing this book.